INSTANT POT
COOKBOOK
FOR BEGINNERS

DELICIOUS QUICK AND EASY EVERYDAY MEAL
FOR BEGINNERS AND ADVANCED USERS

BY

NAOMI LAKEN

ISBN: 978-1-950284-64-1

INSTANT POT
COOKBOOK
FOR BEGINNERS

Delicious Quick and Easy Everyday Meal for Beginners and Advanced Users.

Slow Cooker → Instant Pot

Slow Cooker to Instant Pot Conversion Chart Included

INSTANT POT COOKBOOK

NAOMI LAKEN

ISBN: 978-1-950284-64-1

Disclaimer

Please note, the information contained in this book, are for educational purposes only. Every attempt has been made to provide accurate, up to date and reliable complete information. By reading this document, the reader agrees that under no circumstances are we responsible for any losses, direct or indirect, which are incurred as a result of the use of the information contained in this document, including but not limited to errors, omissions or inaccuracies.

Table of Contents

<u>INTRODUCTION</u>

What is in cooking beyond ingredients? Many used to believe that once you get your ingredients in the right quantities according to the recipes, you're good to go. Little did they know that a lot more is involved in having a great meal. I'm sure this is going to be an eye-opener for a lot of people.

Beyond having the right mixture of ingredients, you also need crucial culinary skills to handle your recipes aright. It is ultimately important to know when and how to add each ingredient to achieve a specific taste or flavor. Even at that, you may still not get it just right.

The best and most experienced cooks, including even the cordon bleu together with the commis chefs, depend greatly on their tools to serve the exciting meals that they're being praised for. (Let's help them refer to their tools and equipment as utensils.)

It is good to now focus on one of those tools that separate two equally-skillful kitchen mayors. That's the Instant Pot. The pots that come in various sizes and models have warmed their ways into the hearts and minds of those who could do anything to prepare a sumptuous meal that will be pleasant to their taste buds and those of their family and friends.

But you will be particularly excited about how the cookbook begins. It beings by telling you all you have to know about the Instant Pot. In the chapter introducing you to the Instant Pot, you will come across the basics of pressure cooking and its benefits. I'm sure you will have some more appreciation for the Instant Pot after reading about how it works.

I have seen a lot of cookbooks about freely referring to parts of the pot and its function keys. These authors presume that all users are familiar with all that. The release methods of the Instant Pot also deserve to be explained. All these are discussed in the first chapter of this book. You can then continue to browse through the recipes of your choice as they've been well categorized in subsequent chapters.

Many readers will especially appreciate the glossary at the end of this book. It includes explanations about measurement units, conversions, and abbreviations.

It is instructive at this stage to tell you that there are about 20 different models and sizes of the Instant Pot that you can choose from. The size ranges from 3 to 8 quarts. All recipes you'll read about in this book will be based on what you can cook in the 3-quart size Instant Pot. This is the ideal pot for a couple or a small family of two to three.

I sincerely hope that this eBook will perfect your cooking as it enhances your skills.

CHAPTER 1: PRESSURE COOKING AND THE INSTANT POT BASICS

The art of cooking is as old as the existence of humanity. Thus, it's expected to be changing with times and seasons. It had experienced tremendous changes over time, and in quick successions in recent decades. After the pressure cooking has taken the stage now, the world has been seeing it has never been seen in cooking.

What are we talking about here?

What Is Pressure Cooking?

Pressure cooking refers to cooking foods at high pressure in a sealed cooking utensil now generally being referred to as the pressure cooker. You can use either water or another cooking liquid that is water-based. The science of this is that boiling is limited by the high pressure while the cooking temperature can go up to around 212°F to 250°F.

Pressure cooker operates on a basic principle, namely steam pressure. Once you apply heat to an airtight pressure cooker, there will be a lot of steam inside it. It's this heat that builds up high pressure which ends up cooking the food inside the pot faster.

The Frenchman Denis Papin is believed to have invented the pressure cooker in the 1600s. As a renowned physicist, he set at translating his discoveries in physics into cooking, using the technology we now study as pressure and steam. Of course, Papin was one of the fathers of the current steam technologies due to his famous studies in steam.

The first pot he made in 1679 was named the "Steam Digester". It actually served his purpose of reducing the cooking time for a great number of foods, though the airtight cooker was deficient in safety, even as when he presented it as a scientific study to the Royal Society of London in 1861. After a while, with some improvements and enhancements with the use of better technology, the first pot passed the safety test.

Other scientists like Georg Gutbrod based in Stuttgart, Germany in 1864 continued where Papin stopped. In 1919, José Alix Martínez a Spaniard from Zaragoza got the patent for pressure cooking. And in 1938 and 1939, during the New York World's Trade Fair, the great scientist, Alfred Vischer also presented his pressured cooker invention.

The foundation was thus laid for the successive generations of pressure cookers. The cookers of decades ago were far cry from what is being sold in markets today. Times, enlightenments, and discoveries have changed things over. Throughout the ages, three to four generations of pressure cookers have been identified. These are based on the timers they integrate and their control capability.

The first generation is the electric pressure cooker with a kind of mechanical timer. This generation of pressure cookers doesn't incorporate delayed cooking capability. But it's the pioneer of the safety measured introduced into the cooking with pressure cookers.

The second generation is the electric pressure cooker with a digital controller. This introduced delayed cooking and had a controller that displays a countdown timer while the pressure is graduating to the set one. It's the generation of pressure cookers that take the cooking to the next level. It introduced sensors that detect, among others, the improper placing of the lid.

Then, we have the third generation electric pressure cooker. This one comes with smart programming that includes preset cooking times. This and other settings are based on the heating intensity, duration, pressure, and temperature. It also adds more to the safety and convenience of this device, making cooking fun and enjoyable. All the modern Instant Pots in markets belong to the third generation.

Yet, there is the fourth generation electric pressure cooker. This is known as the connected cooker. The main deviation of this from the third generation is that it brings the control panel right to your hands. It can be connected to a Bluetooth device and Wi-Fi. There apps that can be installed on your smartphone through which you can control your cooking.

A pressure cooker that is currently in vogue is the Instant Pot. It has brought great innovation to the world of cooking. Well, what is it really?

What Is an Instant Pot?

The Instant Pot is a brainchild of a team of veteran food technologists from Canada who brainstormed on solutions that will serve the interest of those leading busy lifestyles so that they could be cooking at home in spite of their busy schedule. That is why it's called the Canadian brand of kitchen electronic appliances. These veterans were among the professionals who were hard-pressed for the time to spend in cooking.

They needed what can help them to prepare quality and delicious meals to their taste in less time. They could thus stop consuming fast foods and junks outside and instead eat conveniently at home. After 18 exhausting months of intense research, design, and development, they came up with the current kitchen companion in the name of the Instant Pot.

The Instant Pot is a programmable pressure cooker developed with a sophisticated microprocessor. But it's more than just a pressure cooker. It combines all the functions of a rice cooker, slow cooker, steamer, and a warmer. This is quite an unparalleled innovation.

While the manufacturers launched the product as five cooking appliances in one, it has continued to grow beyond that. It successfully stands in also for the deep fryer, yogurt cooker, and a lot more. At some point, it was described as a 7-in-1 appliance, and even 9-in-1 at other times and the team of manufactures has not rested on its oars. Up till this moment, research and development are still ongoing to make the Instant Pot a better thing.

How the Instant Pot Works

The Instant Pot looks like any other regular pot or pressure cooker. But there are a few definitive differences. The Instant Pot has a modified lid which that creates a seal on the pot by locking on over a rubber gasket. With this sealing, the cooker traps the heat and raises the temperature of the boiling water. That's what speeds up the boiling, braising, or steaming of water.

You need to add a minimum of one cup of water or other liquid to the food you intend cooking in the pressure cooker in order to produce sufficient steam pressure. As the high heat is applied the pressure trapped in the pot that cannot escape because the lid is locked in place, the atmospheric pressure inside the cooker will increase by 15 psi.

Once this pressure is increased by 15 pounds above the normal sea level, the water boiling point goes to 212°F to 250°F. And the higher the temperature, the faster the food cooks. But there are electric pressure cookers that have a lower setting than 15 psi. You can use a lower setting like 10 or 11 psi, which is about 235°F for delicate foods. There are pressure cookers that you can program to graduate from the low temperature that you use to soak beans and whole grains, to higher temperatures that you cook on.

There usually is a gauge or a pop-up rod on top of the lid that gives an indication when the pot has reached the full pressure. The release valve is opened and allows the steam out in a regulated flow. This helps to maintain the pot's constant pressure.

In summary, the Instant Pot works with steam pressure. As a sealed pot that traps a lot of steam, it builds up high pressure when being heated and this is what cooks your food faster. There are two basic effects of this pressure steam. First, it raises the boiling point of the water in the pot from the maximum 212°F in a regular pot to the as high as 250°F. The second effect is that the pressure forces liquid and moisture into your food more quickly and keeps it there. This also contributes to the speed of cooking. An extra effect of the extra-high heat is that it aids browning or caramelizing excellently.

Benefits of Pressure Cooking

The following are the benefits of pressure cooking:

- **Energy and time saving**

Besides microwaves, no other cooker saves time and energy like the pressure cooker. Two factors are responsible for this. It doesn't exert much energy because the inner is fully insulated and can trap up the heat. Secondly, it requires far less amount of liquid than other pots. This allows it to boil faster. Using pressure cooking, you can cut down on time and energy usage by up to 70%.

- **Retention of vitamins and nutrients**

Water-soluble vitamins in your foods are retained when you pressure cook your meals. Thus, meals can keep their nutritional value. This doesn't happen when you cook with conventional pots. But with deep, quick, and even cooking of a pressure cooker, you can be sure of retaining as much as 90 percent of the water-soluble vitamins in the food. This is due to its use of less water.

- **Helping to preserve the food's taste and appearance**

Oxygen and excessive heat that the foods get exposed to can alter the tastes and dull the colors of your food when you cook in open containers. This will happen even when you use containers with a lid but that are not airtight. But the pressure cooker doesn't let in oxygen. The steam cooking will thus help retain the food's brightness of colors and phytochemicals. And flavors will develop faster and more profoundly.

- **Elimination of harmful microorganisms and naturally occurring toxins**

Most microorganisms will die at or before reaching 212°F. But some dogged ones can survive that temperature and come back active. Pressure cookers boil water at higher temperature as it has been seen. There's no chance for any microbes to survive. That's why it can be the nursing mothers' preference for sterilization of jars, baby bottles, and water. Besides, there are some naturally occurring toxins like phytohaemagglutinin that can be found in some foods if not well cooked. There are also aflatoxins which are a mold-based mycotoxin. Then can occur when beans, corn, and rice are wrongly stored or exposed to humidity. With boiling above 212°F, these and similar toxins will be neutralized.

- **It is convenient**

The convenience of pressure cooking is due to its preset smart programs for common cooking tasks like the following and a lot more.

1. Soup
2. Meat & Stew
3. Beans & Chili
4. Poultry
5. Slow cook
6. Yogurt
7. Steaming
8. Congee/Porridge
9. Multigrain

10. Rice
11. Sauté/Browning
12. Keep warm

Another source of its convenience is intelligent programming. The Instant Pot pressure cooker has one-touch programs that are capable of producing consistency of cooking results. You can fine-tune the programs further to your preference. You can also save the setting for the pot to remember the adjustment the next time.

Its automatic cooking also adds to the convenience. The cooking process of the Instant Pot is fully automated such that each step of the cooking task has been timed. If you choose the automated cooking, the cooker will switch from preheating and continue the cook cycle and end it all at "Keep Warm" at the completion of the cooking.

The convenience is also produced by the pressure cooker's ability to delay cooking by up to 24 hours. It helps a lot in planning meals. You're not compelled to refrigerate foods that not freezing-compatible like beans, potatoes, and rice.

- **It makes your meals tender and flavorful**

The pressure cookers' embedded processors' advanced technology enables them to cook foods deeply and evenly. This exerts a measure of control over cooking cycles. The airtight environment that seals up the meal also traps in the vitamins, nutrients, and flavors. This automatically brings out the meal's best taste. But beyond that, tougher cuts of meat succumb easily to the steam pressure from the pressure cooker. When the meat breaks down completely, you can have tender fall-off-the-bone meat.

- **It cooks consistently**

Again, thanks to the intelligent programming, it cooks consistently regardless of the volume of food. For instance, the duration for the cooking of one egg is the same with the cooking of one dozen of eggs. The only difference is the quantity of water.

- **Clean and pleasant kitchen and cooking**

Using the instant pot, you don't have to contend with any ugly spew on the lid of your pot or the kitchen countertop. The airtight sleek pot keeps everything inside and does so noiselessly. And your house is free from aroma and flavor until the food is served as everything is locked in. You don't have a lot to clean up since you don't have to set up an array of appliances; remember that it's an all-in-one appliance. It saves, not only your cooking and cleaning time, but also your money. It keeps your kitchen uncluttered and organized.

Instant Pot Pressure Cooking Basics, Tips and Precautions

Operation

➢ *Safety Tip:* Pressure cookers are generally safe and easy to use. Being a pressure cooker doesn't imply any difficulty. It's just that the food in the Instant Pot pressure cooker cooks hotter and faster.

➢ *Cooking frozen foods:* You don't have to thaw foods before cooking them in the pressure cooker. And by the way, who has the time for that. However, note that it will take a bit longer to reach pressure since you're starting with a cooler temperature.

➢ *Cooking time:* Your recipe cooking time shouldn't be seen as the total time it takes for you do the cooking. How do you account for the time before reaching pressure? And what about the time for pressure release? These are just two examples.

➢ *Size, not the weight, matters to timing:* The chunk of foods with less weight will take longer to cook than small cut foods with more weight. It goes this way smaller cuts = less cook time.

➢ *The timer needs to be understood:* It can be somewhat baffling. The countdown will not start until the Instant Pot reaches the pressure of 15 psi. You also need to realize that the timer will start counting up automatically after a series of beeping. This time counts for the natural pressure release.

➢ *There should be a sufficient amount of liquid:* At least, one cup of liquid should be in the Instant Pot at all times. Otherwise, you may not get those beautiful results that you've read about. After all, it's called a pressure cooker which needs steam. And it's the combination of water and heat that produces steam.

➢ *Vent knob tip:* The vent valve (vent knob) is unsteady and for good reasons. It must always be in the "sealing" position while cooking if all the benefits of the Instant Pot are to be realized. But you can set it to "venting" if you want the steam to escape from the pot. It is also known as the steam/pressure release valve or handle.

➢ *Cooking pot in pot is possible:* You can do the PIP method. If the timing and pressure are the same, you can make, for example, bread and rice in the same pot at the same time. Just insert another pan inside the pot while the different kinds of food will not have any contact. Please make sure the insert is oven safe; it's automatically IP safe.

➢ *Sealing ring:* It may seem like "don't touch" if you don't want to damage it. But removing sealing rings doesn't necessarily damage the press, especially if it has to be cleaned. Some savory foods can leave their scent in the ring, but it will go with repeated use and cleaning. Some people choose to have different sealing rings for different foods producing different scents.

> *A one-pot wonder:* You can brown your meat, add sauce and veggies, and cook all in one pot.

Cleaning Tips

You need to learn how to clean and set up your Instant Pot pressure cooker. First, clean the exterior housing of the pot with a damp cloth to remove any food residual or stain. Clean the rim with foam or brush as it can sometimes be quite hard to wipe. But this may not be regularly needed.

Secondly, clean the pot liner. This stainless steel inner pot is dishwasher safe, so you don't have to worry. But you can also hand wash it using warm water with soap. Some cloudiness or discoloration may build up with time. Rainbow color can even build up in the bottom part of the inner pot. It's a normal thing to happen with time and repeated usage. You can use white vinegar to clean this. Common dish stain removers can deal effectively and safely with tougher stains.

The lid and parts do not usually require strenuous cleaning. It needs just a quick rinse under running water after each use. If you need to remove some splattered food or liquid, wash by hand using warm water with soap. It's not advisable to wash it in the dishwasher. You rarely need to wash other parts. However, if you have to, you can carefully remove them and install them back into the position.

The washing of the sealing ring requires extra care. This is because its role is the most crucial in the cooking process. Reduce the frequency of pulling out the ring for washing. You may end up stretching or deforming it if care is not taken.

Precautions

> *Avoid overcooking*: The Instant Pot has the tendency to overcook veggies. High heat plus steam is not nice for broccoli, Brussels sprouts, kale, mushrooms, and zucchini among other vegetables. If you have to cook them in high heat, use the QR rather than NPR.
> *Don't use it in small kitchens*: It's not quite compatible with a small kitchen. You won't be able to use it a quick pressure release if your kitchen is lacking in space. You need a bigger counter or storage space.
> *Watch out for lead poisoning:* There's minimal danger of lead poisoning. Some tests have found that some trace amounts of lead are in the older models of the Instant Pot. But the parts and areas having any contact with food are completely lead-free.
> *Watch liquid usage:* Still on liquid; it's important to stress that while the liquid is important to the functionality of your pressure cooker, you should also understand too much liquid is detrimental to the taste of your food. Be aware also that very little amount of evaporation takes place in the pressure cooker.

Much of the water you add will be retained in the finished food. You may end up with a dish lacking flavor or a sauce too thin. If you don't want to pull the flavor out of the food, you generally don't need more than half a cup to one cup of liquid to have a well-cooked meal. Unless otherwise indicated in the recipe, stick with a little amount of water.

➤ *Avoid overloading:* Don't overfill the pressure cooker. Your Instant Pot is not meant to be filled with ingredients. If you have to pack in your ingredients too tight, you've overloaded your cooker. This leads to uneven cooking. In fact, it can take too long to come to pressure, if it will ever come to it at all. Remember that some foods like beans and rice can expand, so don't fill the pot with them more than halfway. On no condition should any food fill the cooker beyond two-thirds full. This creates the needed space in your pot to function.

➤ *Don't cook the foods all at once:* You may be tempted to throw in all the ingredients at once. That will be a grave mistake as some parts of your food will overcook while others will not cook well. You need to realize, for example, that, meats and vegetables have different cook times. As you will see in the recipe instructions, you need to cook your food separately if the cook times vary significantly. You can start with large cut ingredients or meat and release the pressure. Then add small cuts, veggies, and tender ingredients. You may then resume the final stage.

➤ *Carefully add the thickeners:* Pressure cooker works on the steam pulled from the liquid trapped inside. It may not form well if you add thickeners like cornstarch or roux to a thick sauce.

Parts of the Instant Pot

There are three main components of the Instant Pot. They are:
1. The inner pot
2. The cooker base, and
3. The lid

Each of these components has small parts that perform crucial functions. Let's go through each of them.

Inner Pot
This is a removable vessel inside the main pot and it's used for cooking. When the liquid inside the inner pot boils, it turns into steam. It's the buildup of this steam that creates pressure. The Instant Pot's inner pot is made with a high-quality 304 food grade which is 18/8 stainless steel.

Trivet: Inside the main pot is also a silver rack called trivet or steam rack. Foods can be placed on this rack to cook if they don't need to have any direct contact with the bottom of the pot. Food on the trivet will be above the water level.

Cooker Base

This is the housing for the microprocessor, a heating element, sensors, and the control panel. In the third generation of the pressure cooker, the microprocessor is at the core. Working with the built-in sensors, it monitors and automatically regulates the pressure and temperature of the electric cooker on the basis of the selected smart program.

The cooker base engages the heating element in order to keep the temperature and the level of pressure stable. If anything unsafe is detected, the cooker will send the error signal by creating a beep. The power supply will then be cut off from the heating elements.

The Lid

The Instant Pot lid is made of strong 201 stainless steel (food grade). It uses both steel braces and locking mechanism. This is what prevents the lid from being flung open by the pressure from within while it's cooking. Due to the activities of the microprocessor, the power supply to the heating element will be cut off if the lid is not fully locked.

Several small parts of the lid contribute to the proper sealing and regulating of pressure. They are:

> *Steam release:* Over the years, the designs of steam release (pressure release valve) have changed with different models. In all cases, it has two settings namely "Venting" and Sealed." While the former allows the steam to escape, the latter traps the steam in the inner pot for the pressure to build.

> *Sealing ring:* It is made from long-lasting silicone rubber. When the steam release is set to "Sealed" after the lid is closed, there will be pressure from the lid and the inner pot on the ring so that it can create an airtight seal. Thus, the pressure can safely build up in response to the applied heat.

> *Float valve and silicone cap:* The float valve functions as the latch lock that prevents the lid from turning. As the pressure starts building up in the inner pot, the float valve will be pushed up. This forces the silicone cap to fully seal the cooker. So the lid remains intact and doesn't turn even with the force applied.

> *Anti-block shield:* This is the stainless steel cover that protects the steam release pipe from clogs by food particles. This enhances the steady release of steam during vent release.

Instant Pot Function Keys Usage Guide

There are several function keys on the Instant Pot pressure cooker. You don't have to be scared about what each of them does. Some keys might have slightly different labeling on different models. But below is a general guide to the use of each of those keys.

1. Manual / Pressure: This is probably the most often used key on the Instant Pot. For those who aren't sure of the cook program to set, this button gives users the opportunity to pressure cook while manually selecting the cooking time. It allows you to set the pot to the desired pressure, temperature, and time by using the "+/-" buttons. This will depend on the recipes and notes regarding the meals to cook at high or low pressure. Anything around 10.2 to 11.6 psi and 239°F to 244°F is recognized to be "High Pressure" while "Low Pressure" something around 5.8 to 7.2 psi and 229 to 233°F.

2. Sauté: This is the second commonest button on the Instant Pot in order of usage frequency for most users. Almost anything can be sautéed and produce the same result as you would get if cooking in an open pan or skillet. Using the "Sauté" button, you're not bound by the rule of having a specified amount of water in the pot because you're not pressure cooking. The sauté temperature can be adjusted to the range of Normal mode (320°F to 349°F), More mode (347°F to 410°F), and Less mode (275°F to 302°F).

3. Slow Cook: This is the button you use if you want your Instant Pot to serve as a slow cooker. Just add your food as if you're adding it to a slow cooker, close the lid, and press the "Slow Cook" button. The default cook time when using the slow cook option is 4 hours. But you can use "+/-" buttons to set the cook time to your desired time.

5. Keep Warm / Cancel: When the cooking is done and you're not ready to serve it, the "Keep Warm" / "Cancel" function on the Instant Pot will stop the cooking and keep your food warm for up to 99 hours. It will keep counting up the number of minutes or hours that your food has been kept on the "Keep Warm" / "Cancel" mode. For example, the display panel will display something like "L3:30" if the cooking has stopped for 3 hours, 30 minutes. Your food will be kept at the temperature of between 145° F to 172°F. The function key is also used to cancel a wrong option you just selected and return your Instant Pot to the standby mode.

6. Bean / Chili: This is the button you need to use if you're cooking the normally time-consuming foods like beans and legumes. It makes the cooking of such foods as black beans and kidney beans faster (10-15 minutes and 20-25 minutes respectively). The default cook is a High Pressure of 30 minutes. However, it can be adjusted for "More" to "High Pressure" for 40 minutes and "Less" to "High Pressure" for 25 minutes.

7. Meat / Stew: The default setting when you use this button is High Pressure for 35 minutes. It's the Instant Pot setting for cooking stew or meat dish. If you want fall-off-bone meat, you can set it to "More" to have the "High Pressure" for 45 minutes. It can also be set to "Less" for 20 minutes High Pressure.

8. Multigrain: If you're cooking brown rice and wild rice which takes longer than white rice to cook, this is the best setting. The rice to water ratio for brown rice should be 1:1.25 while that for water and wild rice is 1:3. The default pressure cooking time for this setting is 40 minutes at "Normal." If you need to, you can adjust it as needed to "Less" for 20 minutes of pressure cooking time. It can also be adjusted to "More" at 45 minutes of cook time.

9. Porridge: This is the best setting to cook rice porridge and other grains porridges. The default cook time is 20 minutes at High Pressure. But it can be adjusted to "More" for 30 minutes of High Pressure or to "Less" for 15 minutes of High Pressure. Please note that it's better to use NR when using the "Porridge" setting. The porridge may be splattered through the steam release vent if you use QR.

10. *Poultry:* Chicken and Turkey recipes do well with the "Poultry" button which defaults to a High Pressure at 15 minutes. It can be adjusted to "More" for 30 minutes of High Pressure or to "Less" for 5 minutes of High Pressure.

11. *Rice:* Cooking rice in the Instant Pot using the rice button reduces the cook time by half the time it takes to cook in a conventional rice cooker. Most rice can be cooked on the "Rice" setting in about 4 to 8 minutes. This function key automatically adjusts the cook time by the quantity of food in the unit.

12. *Soup:* If you want to prepare a broth, soup, or stock, this is the function key that will do that for you. Once you press the button, the Instant Pot microprocessor will regulate the pressure and temperature so that the liquid doesn't boil too much. This setting too also allows the pressure to be adjusted to either low or high which moves the time between 20-40 minutes.

13. *Steam:* This is the button that enables you to steam seafood and vegetables in your Instant Pot. If you don't want to reheat your food with microwaving, you can use the Steam function using the stream rack so that your food doesn't burn or stick to the inner pot's bottom. For a more definite timing, you can use the "+" or "-" button.

14. *Timer Button:* It's a versatile button on the Instant Pot. It's used to delay the cooking. Press the timer button and adjust the delayed hours using "+/- " buttons and wait a second before pressing the "Timer" again. You can cancel the set time by pressing the "Keep Warm / Cancel" button as usual.

Instant Pot Pressure Release Methods Explained

In virtually all the Instant Pot recipes you'll come across, you'll find reference being made to the Natural Pressure Release and Quick Pressure Release. What do those expressions mean?

These refer to the two methods or allowing the steam pressure that cooks your food to be released before you open the lid. You surely don't need to be reminded that pressure cookers shouldn't be opened with the pressure inside.

1. *Natural Pressure Release:* When the cooking stops and the pot starts to cool, it will gradually release all the pressure built up inside naturally. The pressure will get out through the vent and pin located on the lid top. That's what's referred to as Natural Pressure Release. The duration of the natural pressure release will be determined by the quantity of food and the length of cook time.

2. *Quick Pressure Release:* It's also being referred to as manual pressure release. This is what you do when you don't want to wait for the pressure to release naturally. Rather, you

carefully flip the knob from "Sealing" to "Venting" before the pot cools down naturally. Many recipe instructions will recommend that you can do a quick release of pressure or manually release it after some specified minutes of the natural pressure release.

Anytime you're doing a quick or manual release of pressure, you need to exercise some cautions. Use an oven mitt or a long-handled spoon to avoid being burnt while releasing the steam. You can also direct the vent valve away from your cabinet so that steam doesn't spoil it or splash back.

Now let's go to the recipes for two.

CHAPTER 2: THE INSTANT POT BREAKFAST RECIPES FOR BEGINNERS

If breakfast is truly the most important meal of the day as being posited by nutrition experts, it deserves to be cooked in the Instant Pot. What if you're not ready to freeze any food remnant to be thawed later? You need to look in the direction of the Instant Pot breakfast recipe for two – PERFECT for beginners. This chapter contains more than enough of such recipes.

Apple Cinnamon Oat Porridge

- **Prep Time:**   10 minutes
- **Cook Time:**   15 minutes
- **Passive Time:**   10 minutes
- **Yields:**   2 servings

Ingredients

- ¾ cup old-fashioned oats (rolled)
- ¾ cups milk
- 1 ¾ cups water (to be divided)
- ½ cinnamon stick (¼ inch)
- 2 tbsps. brown sugar
- 1 apple (to be finely chopped, divided)
- ½ tsp. cinnamon (ground)
- ¼ cup walnuts (roughly chopped)

Instructions (for cooking the oats)

1. Mix the oats, 1 cup of water, and cinnamon stick together in a small bowl that is Instant Pot compatible and can fit inside your IP. Then pour in the remaining ¾ cup of water into the pot with the trivet placed inside.
2. Place the bowl containing the mixture on the trivet inside the pot and lock the lid into place.
3. Press the "Pressure Cook" / "Manual" button and use the "+/-" key to adjust the pressure to "High" and set the time to 5 minutes. Check to see that the steam release knob is in the "Sealed" position.
4. When it beeps to signal that the cooking is done, allow the NPR for 10 minutes and then do the QR to get the remaining pressure out.

Instructions (for assembling the oats)

1. Carefully unlatch to remove the lid. Take the bowl out of the IP and mix in cooked oat thoroughly. Then stir in sugar, ½ of the chopped apple, cinnamon, and chopped walnut. Top with the remaining ½ of the apple and serve immediately.

Eggs "en Cocotte"

- **Prep Time:**   5 minutes
- **Cook Time:**   16 minutes
- **Yields:**   2 servings

Ingredients

- 1 tbsp. unsalted butter
- 1 tsp. extra-virgin olive oil
- 4 white button (or cremini mushrooms, to be halved and sliced)
- 1 tbsp. chopped onion
- ½ cup stock (vegetable or mushroom)
- ½ cup heavy cream whipping
- 1 tbsp. sherry (dry)
- ½ tsp. kosher salt (or to taste)
- Pinch of black pepper (freshly ground)
- 2 large eggs
- 2 tbsps. cheddar cheese (grated, sharp)
- 1 tbsp. chopped fresh chives (to garnish)

Instructions

1. Press the "Sauté" button on the IP and adjust it to "Medium Heat". Melt the butter in the inner pot and add the olive oil. Allow it to heat until it's foaming.
2. Add mushrooms and stir occasionally as it cooks for about 5 minutes or until all the liquid in the mushrooms is released. Add the chopped onion and cook until soft, usually about 4 minutes.
3. Add the cream, sherry, and stock and stir. Allow to cook for about 5 minutes for the liquid to dry and reduce to about half. Then stir in the pepper and salt.
4. Divide the mixture into two ramekins. Break an egg each into the ramekins and sprinkle the mixture with the cheddar cheese.
5. Clean the inner pot by rinsing and return it to the pot. Pour 1 cup of water into the inner pot with trivet placed inside. Place the ramekins on the trivet uncovered.

6. Firmly lock the lid into place and select "Pressure Cook" / "Manual". Set the pressure to "High" with the timer adjusted to 2 minutes. After cooking, do the quick release of the pressure.
7. Allow the egg cups to cool for 1 e minutes and the serve with chives as garnishes.

Scotch Eggs

- **Prep Time:**   10 minutes
- **Cook Time:**   15 minutes
- **Yields:**   2 servings

Ingredients

- 2 large eggs
- ½ lb. spicy Italian pork sausage patties (ground, formed into four equal-sized)
- ¾ tbsp. olive oil
- ½ cup water

Instructions

1. Pour ice water into a medium bowl and set aside.
2. Position the steam rack in the inner pot of the IP, add 1 cup of water to the pot bottom, and put the eggs on the steam rack.
3. Tightly lock the lid into place and ensure that the steam release valve is on the "Sealing" position. Press the "Pressure Cook" key and cook on High Pressure with the time set for 6 minutes.
4. At the completion of the cooking, allow the NPR for 5 minutes. Then do the QR and open the lid carefully.
5. Transfer the eggs to the ice water bath and allow it cool for 5 minutes. Then, peel and transfer the eggs to a platter. Set aside.
6. Take the steam rack out and remove also the inner pot from the base. Drain it and return to the base.
7. Set the sausage patties on an even surface and place an egg in the center of each patty so that you can wrap each sausage around each egg form into shape when the sausages have covered the eggs.
8. Start the Instant Pot with the "Sauté" function and add the olive oil to the pot when it's hot. Brown the eggs in the pot; each side for about 6 minutes, turning it with the tongs each time. Transfer the browned eggs to a large plate and cancel the cooking.
9. Return the steam rack to the inner pot and pour ½ cup of water to the bottom of the pot.
10. Tightly lock the lid and move the steam release handle to the "Sealing" position. Select "Pressure Cook" / "Manual" and cook on High Pressure for 10 minutes.

11. After it beeps to signal the end of cooking, do the quick release of pressure and then safely open the lid.
12. Use a tong to transfer the scotch eggs to a platter and serve warm.

Fruity Quinoa and Granola Bowls

- **Prep Time:**   2 minutes
- **Cook Time:**   8 minutes
- **Yields:**   2 servings

Ingredients

- ½ cup quinoa (to be rinsed)
- ¾ cups water
- 1 tbsp. maple syrup (plus more for topping, optional)
- ½ tsp. vanilla extract
- ¼ tsp. cinnamon (ground)
- Pinch salt
- 1 cup nondairy milk
- 1 cup granola (any variety)
- 1 cup Fresh Fruit Compote
- Sliced bananas (for topping, optional)
- Toasted walnuts (for topping, optional)

Instructions

1. Add the first 6 six ingredients in the Instant Pot and stir to mix.
2. Lock the lid in place and set the steam release handle to the "Sealing" position. Press the "Manual" / "Pressure Cook" function key and set to High Pressure for 8 minutes.
3. At the end of the cook time, allow 10 minutes of the natural pressure release and then do a quick release of the remaining pressure.
4. After removing the lid stir the quinoa to smooth and add the desired amount of milk for consistency.
5. Serve the quinoa mixture into bowls and top with compote, granola and any other optional toppings.

Miracle Mom Simple Bagels

- **Prep Time:**   10 minutes
- **Cook Time:**   15 minutes
- **Yields:**   2 servings

Ingredients

- ½ cup all-purpose flour
- 1 tsp. baking powder
- ½ tsp. kosher salt
- ½ cup plain Greek yogurt
- 1 egg (beaten)
- 1 tbsp. water
- Sesame seeds (as a topping) or everything bagel seasoning

Instructions

1. Mix flour and baking powder together in a medium bowl and add salt. Add the Greek yogurt and mix well until it forms a dough ball.
2. Sprinkle the flour on an even surface and divide the dough into 2 fairly equal balls.
3. Roll each ball to form a 7-8" rope and join all ends for a bagel shape to form. Place the bagels on a cooking tray.
4. Combine the beaten egg and water in a small bowl. Brush the mixture over the bagels' tops and sides. Sprinkle a lot of toppings onto the top of bagels and press lightly to absorb.
5. Set the drip pan in the cooking chamber bottom and select the "Airfry" option with the pressure adjusted to High and the time set to 12 minutes. Select "Start".
6. Once the display indicates "Add Food", insert the cooking tray in the topmost or bottom position. And when the display indicates, "Turn Food," don't turn the food. Just change the position of the tray.
7. This time keep an eye on the bagels so as to remove them as soon as they turn golden brown.
8. Serve warm and enjoy!

Bacon and Egg Breakfast Pastries

- **Prep Time:**   5 minutes
- **Cook Time:**   20 minutes
- **Yields:**   2 servings

Ingredients

- 4 oz. sheet puff pastry (frozen)
- 1/3 cup cheddar or asiago cheese (or any common one, shredded)

- 2 slices of bacon (cooked and crumbled)
- 2 eggs
- Parsley or chives (for garnish, finely chopped)

Instructions

1. Thaw and unfold the puff pastry according to the package direction on the floured surface. Then cut into 2 squares and place both squares on a cooking tray.
2. Set the drip pan in the cooking chamber bottom. Select "Airfry" on the display panel and set the temperature to 390 degrees. Set the time to 10 or 15 minutes, depending on how thorough you want it to cook. Then select "Start."
3. When the "Add Food" message appears on the display, insert the tray in the center of the cooking chamber and allow it to fry for 5 minutes.
4. Take the pastry out of the chamber after 5 minutes and press down the center of each pastry using a metal spoon. This will form a nest, but be careful to avoid collapsing the sides.
5. Sprinkle into each depression ½ of the cheese and guide it to the side to line the formed set.
6. Sprinkle around the edges of the nest the ½ of the cooked bacon.
7. Gently crack one egg each into the nest and reinsert the tray containing them into the cooking chamber.
8. Ignore the "Turn Food" message when it's displayed on the display panel. When the cooking is complete.
9. Serve warm with chopped parsley or chives as garnishing.

Pumpkin Spice Steel-Cut Oats

- **Prep Time:**   5 minutes
- **Cook Time:**   15 minutes
- **Yields:**   2-3 servings

Ingredients (dry)

- 1 cup steel-cut oats
- ½ tbsp. pumpkin pie spice
- ¼ cup brown sugar
- ¼ tsp. sea salt
- ¼ cup raisins
- ¼ cup roughly chopped walnuts

Ingredients (for cooking and serving)

- 3 cups water
- ½ cup pumpkin purée

Instruction (to prepare)

1. Add the ingredients one after the order as listed in a jar

Instruction (to cook)

1. Add all the ingredients into the Instant Pot and add the water.
2. Mix and stir in the pumpkin purée.
3. Tightly cover, ensuring that the vent valve is turned to the "Sealed" position. Select "Pressure Cook" / "Manual" and cook on High Pressure for 15 minutes.
4. Select "Cancel" when the cooking is done and wait for 10 minutes of natural pressure release. Then manually release the remaining pressure.
5. Serve immediately or allow it to cool a to the desired temperature before serving.

Family Size Buttermilk Pancake

- **Prep Time:**   10 minutes
- **Cook Time:**   50 minutes
- **Yields:**   2-3 servings

Ingredients

- ¾ cups flour
- ½ tsp. baking powder
- ¼ tsp. salt (or to taste)
- ½ cup buttermilk
- 1 tbsp. butter (melted)
- ½ cup water
- 1 large egg
- 1 ½ tbsps. sugar
- 2 tbsps. vegetable shortening (or butter)
- Any favorite pancake topping(s)

Instructions

1. Combine baking powder, flour, and salt in a bowl and whisk together. Also whisk together the butter, buttermilk, eggs, water, and sugar in another mixing bowl. Combine the two mixtures and stir well until well combined.

2. Spread the shortening (or butter if using) in the bottom and up to 2 inches upsides of your Instant Pot and pour in the mixture. Tightly lock the lid into the place and ensure that the vent valve is on the "Sealing" position.
3. Set the cook time for 40 minutes on Low Pressure. (Some Instant Pot models have Cake setting, it can be used instead of Low Pressure).
4. When the cooking ends, allow 10 minutes of natural pressure release and then do Quick Pressure Release of the remaining pressure.
5. Then run a rubber spatula to around the pancake's edge to remove it and transfer it onto a serving plate. Serve by cutting into wedges and add any favorite pancake topping.

Cinnamon Bun Oatmeal

- **Prep Time:**   10 minutes
- **Cook Time:**   20 minutes
- **Yields:**   2-3 servings

Ingredients

- 1 tbsp. butter
- ½ cup steel cut oats
- 2 cups water (warmed)
- 1/4 tsp. kosher salt (or to taste)
- 1/8 + 1/8 cup brown sugar
- 1 tsp. cinnamon
- 1 oz. cream cheese (softened)
- 1 tbsp. powdered sugar
- 1 tsp. milk
- ½ cup raisins
- Additional cinnamon (optional, for garnish)

Instructions

1. Start the Instant Pot on the "Sauté" function and add butter when hot.
2. Add the oats when the butter melts, and keep sautéing. Stir occasionally until slightly toasted and fragrant which is usually about 5 minutes. Add the water and salt to submerge all the oats, stir well to combine.
3. Stop sautéing by pressing the "Cancel" button.
4. Tightly secure the lid with the vent turned to "Sealing".
5. Select the "Manual" / "Pressure Cook" function and use the "+/-" key to program the cooking to 12 minutes.
6. In the meantime, mix 1/8 cup of brown sugar and cinnamon in a small bowl.

7. Then beat cream cheese, powdered sugar, and milk together in a medium bowl and transfer the mixture in a piping bag.
8. When the IP beeps after 12 minutes of cooking time, do a quick-release of the pressure.
9. Pour in raisins and the other 1/8 cup of brown sugar into the oatmeal and stir well to the desired consistency.
10. Serve hot into 2 or 3 bowls (according to the appetite's size) and with the brown sugar mixture sprinkled evenly over each serving.
11. Then top with cream cheese icing forming a spiral.
12. Garnish, if you like, with additional cinnamon.

Fast and Easy Shakshuka

- **Prep Time:**   5 minutes
- **Cook Time:**   5 minutes
- **Yields:**   2-3 servings

Ingredients

- 2 tbsps. coconut oil
- 2 cups cheddar cheese (full-fat, shredded)
- 1 garlic clove (minced)
- ½ tsp. cilantro (dried)
- ½ tsp. cayenne pepper (ground)
- ½ tsp. cumin (ground)
- ½ tsp. oregano (dried)
- ½ tsp. black pepper (freshly ground)
- ½ tsp. kosher salt (or to taste)
- 14 oz. roasted sugar-free tomatoes (1 can or low-sugar)
- 6 eggs

Instructions

1. Start the Instant Pot on the "Sauté" function and add the coconut oil to melt.
2. Add all the remaining ingredients apart from eggs and stir thoroughly.
3. Carefully break the eggs open and add to the mixture and keep the yolks intact but evenly spaced apart.
4. Secure the lid in place, shift the pressure release to "Sealing" and stop the sautéing program by hitting "Cancel".
5. Then select the "Manual" / "Pressure Cook" function and set to cook for 1 minute on High.
6. Immediately the cooking stops, do quick pressures release.
7. Then serve immediately and enjoy.

Classic Strawberry Jam

- **Prep Time:**   30 minutes
- **Cook Time:**   15 minutes
- **Yields:**   2 to 2 ½ cups

Ingredients

- 4 cups strawberries (hulled and quartered)
- 1 ½ cups sugar
- 3 tbsps. lemon juice
- 3 tbsps. water
- 3 tbsps. cornstarch

Instructions

1. In your Instant Pot, mix strawberries and sugar and set aside for 30 minutes for the berries to soften and release juices by maceration.
2. Then, add in lemon juice and stir well to combine.
3. Tightly close the lid and ensure that the vent knob is on the "Sealing" position.
4. Use the display panel to select "Manual" / "Pressure Cook" and the "+/-" function key to program the cooking time for 1 minute.
5. When the cooking ends, do a manual release of pressure.
6. Select "Cancel" to turn off the pot, then choose the "Sauté" function.
7. Add cornstarch to cold water in a small bowl and stir the mixture into the IP. Keep cooking while stirring repeatedly until the desired thickness.
8. Select "Cancel" and turn the pot off. Allow to cook and pour in a container to cool down before using it.

Crispy Frittata Florentine

- **Prep Time:**   5 minutes
- **Cook Time:**   20 minutes
- **Yields:**   2 to 3 servings

Ingredients

- 2 slices bacon (chopped)
- 1 tbsp. oil
- 1 cup. hash browns (frozen)
- 3 eggs
- 1 tbsp. half and half (or milk)

- ½ tsp. mustard powder
- ½ tsp. kosher salt (or to taste)
- ½ cup spinach (fresh, finely chopped)

Instructions

1. Whisk together the eggs and half and half spices (or milk) in a medium bowl and stir in the spinach. Set aside.
2. Select the "Sauté" function on the display panel. Pour the bacon slices into the Instant Pot and cook to crisp.
3. Use a slotted spoon to remove bacon to a plate lined with a paper towel.
4. Then, add the frozen hash browns. Leave in an even layer for 6-8 minutes without stirring.
5. Drizzle with oil. Turn the hash browns over. Allow it to cook for an additional 4-6 minutes without stirring.
6. Select "Cancel" to turn off the pot. Then transfer the hash browns to a plate with any remaining drippings left.
7. Deglaze using a wooden spatula. When the brown bits have been removed from the bottom of the pot, pour in the egg mixture.
8. Then add the hash browns back to the pot. Fold gently and evenly sprinkle the cooked bacon over the top.
9. Close the lick firmly and have the vent closed. Select the "Manual" / "Pressure Cook" function on the display panel. Using the "+/=" key, set the Instant Pot time 1 minute and the cook program to "Low Pressure".
10. After the cooking stops, do a quick-release of pressure. Then serve warm with frittata cut into wedges.

Elvis-Style Steel Cut Oatmeal

- **Prep Time:**   5 minutes
- **Cook Time:**   30 minutes
- **Yields:**   2 - 3 servings

Ingredients

- 1 tbsp. butter
- ¾ cup steel cut oats
- ½ tsp. kosher salt (or to taste)
- ¼ cup brown sugar
- ¼ cup peanut butter
- 1 banana (sliced)
- cinnamon (as desired, for serving)

- half and half or cream (for serving, optional)
- 2 ½ cups water

Instructions

1. Start the Instant Pot on the "Sauté" function on the display panel and add butter to melt.
2. Add the oats when the butter melts and continue sautéing for about 5 minutes; stir often until slightly toasted and fragrant.
3. Pour water and add salt. Stir to combine and have all oats submerged.
4. Then select "Cancel" to turn off the pot.
5. Tightly close the lid and check to see that the vent knob is on the "Sealing" position. Select the "Manual" / "Pressure Cook" function on the display panel. Using the "+/-" keys set the cooking for 12 minutes on High Pressure.
6. When the cooking is done, wait for 10 minutes of natural pressure release. Then do a quick release of the remaining pressure.
7. Open and stir the oatmeal to absorb the remaining liquid. Add the sugar and peanut butter. Stir thoroughly to combine.
8. Serve hot with the banana as a topping. Sprinkle the cinnamon and drizzle half and half, if using.

Bacon and Asiago Egg Bites

- **Prep Time:**   5 minutes
- **Cook Time:**   15 minutes
- **Yields:**   2 servings

Ingredients

- 2 eggs
- ¼ cup asiago cheese (shredded)
- ½ cup cottage cheese
- ¼ cup heavy cream
- ¼ tsp. salt
- ¼ tsp. pepper
- ½ dash hot sauce (optional)
- 2 strips bacon (cooked and crumbled)

Instructions

1. Blend all ingredients except the bacon in an immersion blender until smooth, usually about 15 seconds.

2. Add nonstick spray to the inside of silicone egg mold to coat. Then distribute the bacon into the egg molds evenly. Pour the mixture into over the bacon equally and loosely cover with foil.
3. Add 1 cup of water in the Instant Pot with the steam rack inserted.
4. Then, lower the egg mold carefully onto the steam rack and close the lid securely in place.
5. Select the "Manual" / "Pressure Cook" function on the display panel. Using the "+/-" keys set the cooking for 10 minutes.
6. When the cooking is done, do a quick release of the pressure. Carefully remove the egg mold and allow it cook for about 2-3 minutes.
7. Remove the egg bites from the mold and serve immediately. It can be refrigerated for up to 7 days.

Magic Omelette Potatoes

- **Prep Time:**   5 minutes
- **Cook Time:**   35 minutes
- **Yields:**   2 servings

Ingredients

- ½ cup water
- 1 lb. russet potatoes (2 potatoes total)
- 2 eggs (beaten)
- ¼ cup ham (diced)
- 1 tbsp. red onion (to be diced)
- ½ tbsp. parsley (finely chopped)
- ¼ cup cheese (shredded)
- Salt (to taste)
- Pepper (freshly ground, to taste)

Instructions

1. Slice off the top of potatoes lengthwise and produce an appearance of a lid that is about ½ inch thick at its peak.
2. Add water in the Instant Pot and insert the steam rack and set the potatoes on it.
3. Close the lid securely in place and set the vent knob on the "Sealing" position. Select the "Manual" / "Pressure Cook" function on the display panel. Using the "+/-" keys set the cooking for 12 minutes.
4. When the time is up, do the quick release of the pressure and carefully transfer the potatoes to a cutting board. Allow to cool a bit.

5. Gently scoop out the center of the potatoes flesh but not too deeply so that the potatoes can still be strong enough to stand on their own. Also, don't pierce the skin.

6. In a medium bowl, roughly mash the half of the scooped out potato centers though, it may not be well cooked at this time. (Keep the other half of the centers in case you will still need it.)

7. Add the eggs, ham, 1 tablespoon of cheese, onion, parsley to the potato centers. Stir well to combine.

8. Fill each potato shell with the mixture. Then top with the remaining cheese.

9. Return the potatoes to the steam rack and tightly close the lid in place. Check to be sure that the pressure release knob is on the "Sealing" position. On the display panel, select the "Manual" / "Pressure Cook" function and use the "+/-" key to set the cook time for 6 minutes.

10. After the cooking time, manually release the pressure.

11. You can brown the cheese by setting the potatoes under the broiler. Then serve hot while topping with the ground pepper and salt.

Sausage and Kale Egg Muffins

- **Prep Time:**   5 minutes
- **Cook Time:**   10 minutes
- **Yields:**   2 servings

Ingredients

- 1 tsp. avocado oil
- 2 tsp. bacon fat (or more avocado oil)
- 4 oz. fully cooked chicken sausage (diced)
- 4 small kale leaves (any variety, finely chopped)
- ½ tsp. kosher salt (or to taste)
- ½ tsp. black pepper (ground)
- 4 medium eggs
- ¼ cup heavy whipping cream (or full-fat coconut milk)
- 4 tbsps. shredded white cheddar (optional, or Swiss cheese)
- 1 cup water

Instructions

1. Grease the inside of the four silicone muffin cups all sides, with 1 tablespoon of avocado oil (you can use any of either ceramic ramekins or half-pint mason jars.) If available, a silicone egg bites mold can be used for this recipe.

2. Start the Instant Pot on the "Sauté" mode and add the bacon fat when to melt when the pot is warm. Add the sausage and continue sautéing. After two minutes, add the kale

leaves, pepper, and salt. Continue sautéing for 2 or 3 minutes at most, or until the kale is wilted.

3. In the meantime, lightly beat together the eggs, cream (or coconut milk) in a medium bowl. Add pepper and the remaining ¼ teaspoon of salt.

4. Stop the sautéing by pressing "Cancel". Then divide the kale sausage into the four muffin cups and pour the egg mixture evenly over the sausage mix lightly with a fork. Top with 1 tablespoon of cheese and loosely cover with foil or silicone lids.

5. Add water into the Instant Pot and place the metal steam rack inside. Arrange the four cups on the rack.

6. Tightly secure the lid with the release valve set on the "Sealing" position. Select the "Pressure Cook" / or "Manual" option and use the "+/-" function to set it to 5 minutes cook time.

7. Once the cook time is up and the IP beeps, wait for 10 minutes of natural pressure release. Then do a quick release of the remaining pressure.

8. Transfer the muffin to a plate and serve warm.

CHAPTER 3: THE INSTANT POT SOUPS AND STEWS FOR BEGINNERS

Your busy schedule may seem to leave no chance for you to cook nice soups or stews for your tasty delight. Thanks to the Instant Pot, that is not really the case. Yes, you can do them; make instant soup, stew, or sauce for just two or three of you. Is it Pacific- -, Chinese-, or Italian-styled soups that you're dying to eat? Recipes for them are here in this chapter. You'll also come across recipes for two for minestrones, chowders, cheeses, shrimps, and bisques. They're all here for your consideration and trial in your Instant Pot.

Chinese Dumpling Soup

- **Prep Time:**   5 minutes
- **Cook Time:**   18 minutes
- **Yields:**   3 servings

Ingredients

- 5 cups chicken (or 2 quarts vegetable) broth
- 2 medium scallions (trimmed, thinly sliced)
- 1 slice of any deli smoked ham (½ inch thick, rind removed, meat to be sliced into 2-3 oz. matchsticks)
- 1 tbsp. sodium soy sauce (regular or reduced; or tamari)
- ¼ tsp. ground ginger (dried)
- 12 oz. frozen chicken (Chinese dumplings)

Instructions

1. Start the Instant Pot on the "Sauté" mode and set to "High" or "More" or "Custom 400°F" with the time set for 10 minutes.
2. Add the broth, ginger, scallions, and soy sauce to the Instant Pot and cook. Stir occasionally until the mixture produces many wisps of steam. Add the frozen dumplings and stir well. Then select "Cancel" to stop the sauté function.
3. Lock the lid onto the place and select the "Soup" / "Broth" key for auto programming. You may also select "Pressure Cook" / "Manual" and cook on High using the "+/-" key to time it to 4 minutes while the "Keep Warm" setting is off. Ensure that the vent valve is on "Sealing".
4. When the cook time is up, use the quick pressure release method and unlatch the lid when the pressure is back to normal.
5. Open the pot and stir well to combine.
6. Serve and enjoy with your choice!

Butternut Squash Bisque

- **Prep Time:** 10 minutes
- **Cook Time:** 25 minutes
- **Yields:** 2-3 servings

Ingredients

- 1 lb. frozen butternut squash (peeled and seeded, cut into ½-1-inch cubes)
- 1 cup vegetable (or chicken) broth
- 1tsp. fresh thyme leaves (stemmed, or ½ tsp. dried thyme)
- ¼ tsp. grated nutmeg or (1/8 tsp. ground nutmeg)
- ¼ tsp. table salt (or to taste)
- 1 cup whole (or low-fat) milk
- ¼ cup heavy (or light, but not fat-free) cream
- 2 tbsps. butter (½ stick)
- 2 tbsps. all-purpose flour

Instructions

1. Add the first five ingredients in an Instant Pot. Stir well to combine. Lock the lid onto the pot and ensure that the vent valve is on the "Sealing" position.
2. If you're using Max Pressure Cooker; simply pressure cook for 4 minutes on Max pressure while the "Keep Warm" setting is off.
3. On All Pressure Cooker: select "Soup" / "Broth" or "Pressure Cook" / "Manual" setting and set the time for 5 minutes while having the "Keep Warm" function set to off. Ensure that the vent valve is on the "Sealed" position.
4. Once the cook time is up, do a quick release of the pressure. Unlatch the lid to open the pot. Add the milk and cream and stir well.
5. Insert an immersion blender into the pot and puree the soup. If you're using a covered blender, you may purée in 3 batches. Place a towel over the opening to prevent the hot soup from being spewed onto you due to a build-up of pressure.
6. After pureeing, whichever way, select the "Sauté" function on the pot and set it to "Low", "Less" or "Custom 250°F" and the time to 5 minutes.
7. Stir the soup often as you bring to a simmer. In the meantime, in a microwave-safe small bowl, melt the butter in a 5-second increment on High. Stir in the flour, using a fork to make a thin paste.
8. As the soup simmers, whisk the butter mixture into the pot (DO NOT STIR). Keep whisking for about a minute until the soup is slightly thickened. Then, cancel the "Sauté" function and cool for some minutes.
9. Then serve on anything of choice.

Corn Chowder (or Corn and Crab)

- **Prep Time:**   10 minutes
- **Cook Time:**   20 minutes
- **Yields:**   2 servings

Ingredients

- 1 slice bacon (diced, optional, 1 tbsp. butter can be used instead)
- 1 small onion (diced)
- ¼ cup diced carrots
- ¼ cup celery (diced)
- ¼ cup red bell pepper (diced)
- 2 cups chicken (broth)
- 1 lb. potatoes (diced)
- ¼ tsp. thyme (freshly chopped)
- ½ tsp. salt (or to taste)
- ¼ tsp. pepper
- ¼ tsp. to 1tsp. hot sauce (to taste)
- 1 ½ cups corn (fresh or frozen)
- ½ tsp. sugar (to taste)
- 1 tbsp. cornstarch (optional)
- 1 ½ tbsp. water (optional)
- Cooked crab meat (optional, to taste)
- ¼ cup to ½ cup heavy cream

Instructions

1. Start the Instant Pot on the "Sauté" mode. Add the bacon (if using, or butter) when the message "Hot" is displayed on the panel. Otherwise, add onion and the next 3 ingredients on the list (or add when the bacon is almost crisp). Sauté for 3 minutes and select "Cancel" to stop sautéing.
2. Then add the broth. Deglaze the pot by thoroughly scraping all browned bits from the pot bottom using a wooden spatula. Add potatoes and the next three ingredients and stir well.
3. Secure the lid in place and set the vent valve to the "Sealing" position. Press the "Pressure Cook" / "Manual" button and set the time to 6 minutes using the "+/-" function key.

4. When the pot beeps to signal that the time is up, manually release the pressure by flipping the valve to venting for a QR. Then press "Cancel" to stop the cooking program and open the pot.

5. Press "Sauté" again and add the corn and sugar. After bringing it to boil, bring to simmer for about 2 minutes. Using a potato masher, break up a few of the potatoes.

6. For thicker chowder, stir in the optional cornstarch and water now. Add it in quarter increments and add more as needed to the desired thickness. The optional crab can also be added now. Stir it in and leave to cook for just 1 minute just to reheat the crab. Then press the "Cancel" button.

7. Add the cream to taste. Serve, garnishing with bacon bits, red peppers, or just enjoy!

Tater Tot Soup

- **Prep Time:**   5 minutes
- **Cook Time:**   20 minutes
- **Yields:**   3 servings

Ingredients

- 3 cups chicken broth (or vegetable, ¾ quarts)
- 1 tbsp. butter
- 1 tsp. garlic (to be peeled, minced)
- 1 tsp. dried basil oregano (or thyme)
- ½ tsp. onion powder
- ¼ tsp. ground black pepper
- ½ lb. hash brown cubes (frozen unseasoned, 3 cups, NOT shredded hash browns)
- 2 ½ cups frozen Tater Tots (or ¾ lb. potato puffs)
- 1 cup shredded mild (or 4 oz. sharp cheddar cheese)

Instructions

1. Start the Instant Pot on the "Sauté" function and set for "High", "More", or "Custom 400°F" and use the "+/-"button to set the time for 10 minutes.

2. Meanwhile, stir in the first 6 ingredients one after the other in the Instant Pot. Stir occasionally until wisps of steam start to rise from the liquid. Then stir in the frozen hash brown cubes followed by Tater Tots.

3. Secure the lid in place and select "Pressure Cook" on Max pressure with the time set for 3 minutes and the "Keep Warm" setting off.

4. If it is on the All Pressure Cooker, select "Soup" / "Broil" or "Pressure Cook" / "Manual" and cook on High Pressure for 4 minutes having the "Keep Warm" setting off and the vent valve closed.
5. When the cooking time is up, quickly bring the pressure inside the pot back to normal by manually releasing it for the pin to drop.
6. Then unlatch the lid to open the pot. Pour in the cheese and stir well. Wait for a couple of minutes while the lid is askew over the cooker for the cheese to melt.
7. Stir thoroughly again. Serve hot and enjoy!

Tortilla Soup

- **Prep Time:**   3 minutes
- **Cook Time:**   22 minutes
- **Yields:**   3 servings

Ingredients

- 1 ½ cups red enchilada sauce (about 10-oz. can)
- 1 cup chicken (or vegetable) broth
- ½ tsp. thyme leaves (stemmed fresh or ¼ tsp. dried thyme)
- ¼ tsp. ground cinnamon
- ¼ tsp. ground cumin
- 4 - 6 frozen quesadillas (of any flavor, or gluten-free quesadillas)

Instructions

1. Start with the "Sauté" function and set it for "High", "More," or "Custom 400°F with the time set for 10 minutes.
2. In the Instant Pot, combine the enchilada sauce, chicken (or vegetable) broth, cinnamon, cumin, and thyme. Let it sauté as you stir occasionally. When several wisps of steam start coming up off the sauce, add the frozen quesadillas but don't push them to the bottom of the pot. Don't worry if the sauce doesn't touch the tops of some of the quesadillas. Just lock the lid tightly onto the pot.
3. If cooking on Max Pressure Cookers, pressure cook on Max with the time set for 5 minutes and the "Keep Warm" setting off.
4. If cooking on All Pressure Cookers, select the "Soup" / "Broth" function and cook press "Pressure Cook" / "Manual" on High with the time set for 8 minutes and the "Keep Warm" setting off and vent release valve on the "Sealing" position.
5. When the cook time is up, quickly return the pot's pressure to normal by selecting doing it manually, turning the valve to "Venting". Then open the lid when the pressure is all gone and cut up the quesadillas using kitchen shears. You can also shred them roughly with two forks.
6. Serve by scooping the broth with tortillas bit and their fillings.

Lazy Day Beef Stew (Fresh or Frozen Beef)

- **Prep Time:**   10 minutes
- **Cook Time:**   40 minutes
- **Yields:**   2 servings

Ingredients

- ½ large onion (to be chopped)
- 1 clove garlic (to be minced)
- ¾ cup beef (or chicken) broth
- 1 tbsp. soy sauce
- ½ tbsp. brown sugar
- ½ tbsp. vinegar (of any kind)
- ½ tsp. salt (or to taste)
- ½ tsp. pepper
- ½ - 1 lb. stew beef (frozen or fresh)
- 1 - 3 red-skinned potatoes (to be cut into 1-inch pieces)
- 1 to 2 carrots (to be cut into 1-inch pieces)
- ½ cup frozen peas
- 1 tbsp. cornstarch
- 1 ½ tbsp. water
- 1 tbsp. chopped fresh parsley (optional)

Instructions

1. In an Instant Pot, combine all listed ingredients up to and including the stew beef. Close the lid in place and set the vent valve to the "Sealing" position. Hit the "Pressure Cook" / "Manual" function key and set the time to 20 minutes using the "+/-" button.
2. Meanwhile, cut the potatoes without the skin and the carrots into 1" pieces. Also, prepare slurry by mixing the cornstarch with water and stirring until smooth.
3. When the cook time is up and the pot beeps, wait for 10 minutes of natural release of pressure and do a quick release of the remaining pressure by flipping the valve to "Venting". Take the lid off the pot when the pin drops showing that the pressure is all gone.
4. Add the potatoes and carrots and gradually push them down to be absorbed by the sauce. Return the lid tightly and have the vent valve on the "Sealing" position again. Select the "Pressure Cook" / "Manual" function with the time set to 4 minutes. Once the time is up, do a quick release of pressure to allow the pin to drop and open the pot.
5. Hit the "Cancel" button to return to the "Sauté" mode. Stir well the cornstarch slurry and add half of it to the stew as it is boiling. Allow it boil and keep adding the slurry until your desired thickness.

6. Again, press the "Cancel" button and stir in the peas without too much turning. The pea should be cooked only by the heat of the stew. Add pepper and salt to taste. Add the optional parsley.
7. Serve and enjoy alongside any lazy day meal.

Vegetable Minestrone With Pasta

- **Prep Time:**   10 minutes
- **Cook Time:**   17 minutes
- **Yields:**   2 servings

Ingredients

- 1tbsp. extra-virgin olive oil
- ½ small yellow onion (chopped)
- 1 ½ garlic cloves (minced)
- 2 carrots (to be peeled and sliced)
- 1 celery stalks (to be sliced)
- 3 cups vegetable broth (low sodium)
- ½ tsp. dried oregano
- ½ tsp. dried thyme
- ½ tsp. fine sea salt (or to taste)
- ½ tsp. black pepper (freshly ground)
- 1 bay leaf
- 15 oz. red kidney beans (1 can, drained and rinsed)
- 15 oz. tomatoes (1 can, diced)
- 3 oz. tomato paste (1 can)
- 1 cup macaroni pasta (dried whole-wheat)
- ¼ cup grated parmesan cheese

Instructions

1. Start with the "Sauté" function and add the olive oil to be heated by the IP inner pot. Add the chopped onion, minced garlic, sliced carrots, celery to the hot pot and sauté until vegetables begin to soften; about 3 minutes.
2. Hit "Cancel" setting and add the broth. Deglaze the bot using a wooden spatula by scraping up any browned bits from the bottom of the pot.
3. Add the dried oregano, dried thyme, bay leaf, pepper, and salt and stir to combine.
4. Next, add red kidney beans, tomatoes, and tomato paste. Don't stir so that tomatoes don't get to the bottom of the pot and burn.
5. Tightly lock the lid into place, and select "Pressure Cook" / "Manual" with the pressure set to High. Use the "+/-" button to set the time to 5 minutes and have the steam release knob turned to "Sealing".

6. Once the pot beeps to signify the end of cooking, do the natural pressure release for 10 minutes and quickly release the remaining pressure.
7. Then serve.

Miso Soup With Shiitakes and Snap Peas

- **Prep Time:**   5 minutes
- **Cook Time:**   12 minutes
- **Yields:**   2 servings

Ingredients

- ½ tsp. avocado oil (or other neutral oil)
- 1 clove garlic (finely grated)
- ¼ inch knob ginger (peeled and finely grated)
- 2 oz. fresh shiitake mushrooms (stems removed and thinly sliced)
- 2 cups water
- 1 cup sugar snap peas (4 oz. cut into ½ -inch pieces)
- 1/8 cup white miso paste
- 1 green onion white and tender green parts (thinly sliced)

Instructions

1. Start the Instant Pot on the "Sauté" function and pour the oil when hot.
2. Add garlic and ginger to the heated oil and leave for about 2 minutes. When it starts bubbling, add the mushrooms continue sautéing for 1 minute more for them to start wilting while the ginger and garlic begin browning. Add water and peas and deglaze using a wooden spatula so that any brown bits will be scrapped up from the bottom of the pot. Cover with the glass lid and leave for about 8 minutes to come to simmer.
3. Take off the lid and select the "Cancel" function to turn off the pot.
4. Pour the miso paste in a small bowl and transfer a quarter of the liquid from the pot into the bowl. Mash the miso, rubbing it against the side of the bowl and stir well to let it fully dissolve.
5. Add the miso mixture with the green onions and stir well in the pot to combine.
6. Ladle the mixture into a bowl and serve hot in two plates.

Tuscan Minestrone Soup

- **Prep Time:**   5 minutes
- **Cook Time:**   35 minutes
- **Yields:**   2 servings

Ingredients **(dry ingredients)**

- 1/8 cup dried onion
- ½ tsp. dried garlic
- 1/3 tbsp. Italian herb blend
- 1/8 cup dried celery
- 1/8 cup dried carrot
- 1/3 tsp. sea salt
- 1/8 cup sundried tomatoes (thinly sliced)
- 1/3 cup kidney beans
- ¼ cup orzo pasta (or pasta shells)
- ¼ cup dried kale chips

Ingredients **(for cooking and serving)**
- 3 cups vegetable broth (or water)
- ¾ teaspoons balsamic vinegar

Instructions

1. Start preparation by layering all the dry ingredients in a jar in the listed order.
2. To start cooking, mix all the jarred ingredients together in the Instant Pot and add the broth or water. Stir well to mix.
3. Tightly cover the lid in place and ensure that the vent valve is on the "Sealed" position.
4. Select "Pressure Cook" / "Manual" and set the pressure to High and time for 35 minutes.
5. When the pot beeps at the end of the cooking, allow 5 minutes of natural pressure release and turn the valve to "Venting" for a manual release of the remaining pressure.
6. When the valve drops, open the lid, stir in the vinegar and serve.

Fasolakia (Green Beans and Potatoes in Olive Oil Tomato Sauce)

- **Prep Time:**   10 minutes
- **Cook Time:**   15 minutes
- **Yields:**   2-3 servings

Ingredients

- 5 oz. diced tomatoes (canned)

- 1 cup water
- ¼ cup olive oil extra virgin
- 1/3 medium zucchini (quartered)
- ¼ bunch fresh parsley (to be washed and chopped)
- ½ bunch fresh dill (to be washed and chopped)
- ¼ tsp. oregano (dried)
- ¼ lb. green beans (frozen, stem if fresh)
- 1 small onion (to be thinly sliced)
- 1 potato (quartered)
- ¼ tsp. salt (or to taste)
- ¼ tsp. pepper (or to taste)

Instructions

1. Select the "Sauté" function on the Instant Pot and add the oil.
2. Once the oil is slightly heated, add the diced tomatoes and stir. Then add water. Add zucchini, parsley, and the remaining ingredients in the order listed. Stir as you add each one.
3. Close the lid on the pot and adjust the vent valve to the "Sealing" position.
4. Select the "Manual" / "Pressure Cook" function and set the time to 15 minutes.
5. Once the pot beeps to signal that the cook time is up, do the quick release of the pressure.
6. Serve the sauce and enjoy!

Italian Goulash

- **Prep Time:**   10 minutes
- **Cook Time:**   20 minutes
- **Yields:**   2 servings

Ingredients

- 1/3 lb. ground beef (90/10 lean)
- 1/3 white onion (diced)
- 1 green bell pepper (diced)
- 1/3 tbsp. garlic (chopped)
- ¼ tsp. salt (or to taste)
- ¼ tsp. pepper (or to taste)
- 20 oz. Italian stewed tomatoes (about 1 can)
- 9 oz. tomato sauce (about 1/3 can)

- 1/3 lb. pasta (any of choice)

Instructions

1. Set the Instant Pot to "Sauté" mode and add beef, onion, bell pepper, and garlic. Stir everything and keep sautéing until the meat browns and veggies are tender.
2. Add the tomato sauce and stewed tomatoes. Add pepper and salt to taste. Mix everything well.
3. Stop sautéing by pressing "Cancel". Select the "Manual" / "Pressure Cook" function and set the time to 10 minutes. Cook on High Pressure.
4. Once done with the cooking, wait for 5 minutes of natural release. Then do the quick release of the remaining pressure.
5. To cook the pasta, add the pasta to the sauce and put it on the "Sauté" and keep stirring frequently until the pasta is cooked. Add water as needed to maintain the desired thickness.

Cheesy Ham and Potato Soup

- **Prep Time:**   5 minutes
- **Cook Time:**   25 minutes
- **Yields:**   2-3 servings

Ingredients

- 1 tbsp. butter
- 1 small onion (finely diced)
- 2 cups chicken broth (to be warmed)
- 1 ½ lbs. gold potatoes (cubed)
- 6 oz. cubed ham
- ½ tsp. garlic powder
- ¼ tsp. pepper
- ¼ cup sour cream
- 1 cup shredded sharp cheddar
- Snipped chives (and additional shredded cheese, for serving)

Instructions

1. Start the Instant Pot on the "Sauté" mode and add butter.
2. Once the butter melts, add onion and continue sautéing for 3 - 4 minutes or until the onion is soft.

3. Pour in the broth and use a wooden spoon to deglaze so that the brown bits from the pot's bottom can be scraped up.
4. Add ham, potatoes, garlic powder, and pepper and keep stirring as you add each ingredient.
5. Select "Cancel" to turn the pot off. Secure the lid into the place, ensuring that the valve is on the "Sealing". Press the "Manual" / "Pressure Cook" function on the display panel. And using the "+/-" keys, program the Instant Pot time to 8 minutes.
6. Once the cooker beeps, do a quick release of the pressure.
7. When the pin drops, open the lid and stir well.
8. Then stir in the sour cream until combined.
9. Stir in the cheese gradually. Keep checking as you stir it in to determine when the mixture is thick and creamy enough.
10. Adjust seasonings as needed and top with chives and/or shredded cheese.
11. Enjoy the soup!

Pacific-Style Smoked Salmon Chowder

- **Prep Time:**   1 minute
- **Cook Time:**   25 minutes
- **Yields:**   2-3 servings

Ingredients

- 1 tbsp. butter
- ½ onion (finely diced)
- 1 stalk celery (diced)
- 2 cloves garlic (minced)
- ½ tsp. dried basil
- ¼ tsp. fennel seeds (lightly crushed)
- 1 ½ cups fish (or seafood stock, warmed)
- ½ lb. gold potatoes (cut into ¾ inches dice)
- 7 oz. diced tomatoes (drained)
- 1 tbsp. tomato paste
- 1 tbsp. capers
- 1 bay leaf
- 2 oz. cream cheese (softened and cut into pieces)
- ½ cup heavy cream
- ½ tbsp. old bay seasoning
- 2 oz. shrimp (chopped, you can use salad shrimp)
- 4 oz. thick-cut smoked salmon (cut into bite-sized pieces)

Instructions

1. Spoon the butter into the Instant Pot and press the "Sauté" key on the display panel to melt.
2. Once the butter melts, add celery and onion, stir gently and sauté for about 5 minutes or until soft. Add basil, fennel, and garlic. Stir and cook for about 2 minutes more.
3. Deglaze with the stock, by scraping the brown bits up from the bottom of the pot, using a wooden spoon.
4. Add potatoes, tomatoes and paste, caper, and bay leaf. Stir all together to combine.
5. Add the cream cheese in an even layer to the top without stirring.
6. Now select "Cancel" to turn the pot off. Secure the lid in place the shift the valve to the "Sealing" position.
7. From the display panel, select "Pressure Cook" / "Manual" function. Using the "+/-" key, set the Instant Pot to cook for 4 minutes.
8. Once the cooker beeps for time up, wait for another 4 minutes for the natural release of pressure. Thereafter, do a quick release of the remaining pressure.
9. Once the pin drops, stir well for about 1 minute to allow the cream fully incorporated.
10. Next, add the cream and old bay and stir well to combine.
11. Fold in the shrimp carefully together with the smoked salmon. Heat through as it returns to "Sauté" mode.
12. Stir now and serve hot with the oyster cracker, cracked pepper, or crusty bread.

Beer Cheese Soup

- **Prep Time:**   10 minute
- **Cook Time:**   20 minutes
- **Yields:**   2-3 servings

Ingredients

- 1 slice bacon (chopped)
- 1 tbsp. butter
- ½ small onion (finely diced)
- ¼ cup diced carrots
- ½ cup diced celery
- ¼ cup flour
- 1 cup chicken broth
- ¼ tsp. black pepper
- ¼ tsp. ground mustard
- 1/8 tsp. cayenne (or to taste)
- 4 oz. beer (of choice)
- 4 oz. sharp cheddar cheese (grated)

- ½ cups salted popcorn (for garnish, choose either cheese popcorn or croutons in a pinch)

Instructions

1. Start by sautéing bacon in the Instant Pot by selecting the "Sauté" function on the display panel until the bacon is crisp.
2. Use a slotted spoon to remove the bacon from the pot onto a plate lined with a paper towel. Set aside.
3. Combine butter, diced onion, carrots, and celery to the bacon drippings. Sauté for about 4 minutes or until slightly softened.
4. Meanwhile, coat the vegetables with flour by sprinkling it on top and stirring.
5. Pour broth into the pot and using a wooden spatula, deglaze, scraping the brown bits from the bottom of the pot.
6. Add black pepper, ground mustard, cayenne, and beer and stir well in the pot to combine.
7. Select "Cancel" to turn the pot off.
8. Secure the lid into place with the vent closed. Select the "Pressure Cook" / "Manual" on the display panel and set the cook time for 7 minutes using the "+/-" keys.
9. When the cooker beeps, wait for 4 minutes of natural pressure release and manually release the remaining pressure. Be careful to avoid any starch spray.
10. Use an immersion blender to puree the vegetable mixture to smooth (you may also use a high-capacity blender).
11. Gradually stir in the cheese in batches while checking for thickness and creaminess.
12. Adjust seasonings as desired and top with bacon and popcorn. Serve hot.

Fireside Tomato Soup

Prep Time: 10 minute

Cook Time: 25 minutes

Yields: 2-3 servings

Ingredients

- ¼ cup fresh basil leaves (loosely packed, chopped)
- ½ tsp. granulated sugar
- 1 ½ - ¾ cups chicken (or vegetable) broth (ready to use, reduced-sodium)
- 15 oz. diced tomatoes with garlic and onion (2 cans, with juice)
- ½ cup half-and-half cream (10%)
- 1/8 cup butter (softened)

- Black pepper (freshly ground)

Instructions

1. Add basil leaves, sugar, broth, and diced tomatoes with juice to the instant pot without stirring.
2. Tightly close the lid and ensure that the steam release handle is turned to "Sealing". Select "Pressure Cook" / "Manual" on the Instant Pot and cook and High for 5 minutes.
3. When the pot beeps, select "Cancel" and allow the natural pressure release for 5 minutes and then do a manual release by turning the valve to "Venting." When the float valve drops, open the lid.
4. Insert an immersion blender to purée the mixture until smooth.
5. Return the Instant Pot to Sauté on Less. Add the cream and butter and cook for 3 minutes, stirring occasionally.
6. Season with pepper to taste and serve.

CHAPTER 4: THE INSTANT POT BEEF, PORK, AND LAMB FOR BEGINNERS

Meat is an essential part of our meal. And if you are not a vegetarian, you will like to enjoy a moderate amount of meat, if not indulge yourself a bit. But cuts of meat can be tough and sometimes can compel you to move away from them if you're pressed for time. The pressure cooking tech of the Instant Pot is something you can count on in dealing deliciously with your beef, pork, and lamb. This chapter contains various meat recipes for two.

Crustless Meat Lovers Quiche

- **Prep Time:**   5 minutes
- **Cook Time:**   30 minutes
- **Yields:**   2 servings

Ingredients

- ½ cup of water
- 2 large eggs (to be well beaten)
- ¼ cup milk
- 1/8 tsp. salt (or to taste)
- 1/8 tsp. black pepper (or to taste, ground)
- 2 slices bacon (to be cooked and crumbled)
- ½ cup sausage ground (cooked)
- ¼ cup ham (to be diced)
- 1 large green onion (to be chopped)
- ½ cup cheese (shredded)

Instructions

7. Add water to the Instant Pot with the metal trivet in the bottom.
8. Whisk together the eggs, milk, pepper, and salt in a medium bowl.
9. Add the bacon slices, sausage, diced ham, onions, and cheese in a soufflé dish and mix well.
10. Pour in the egg mixture, stir to combine.
11. Cover the dish with an aluminum foil. Position the dish on the dish on the trivet inside the pressure cooker using the foil sling.
12. Tightly lock the lid and ensure that the valve is in the "Sealing" position. Choose "Pressure Cook" / "Manual" and cook on High using the "+/-" keys to set 30 minutes cook time.
13. When the timer beeps, allow 10 minutes of natural release and later do a quick release of the remaining pressure.

14. Open the lid and take the dish out. Remove the foil and sprinkle the top with more cheese. And sauté to bring to broil and lightly brown
15. Serve immediately and enjoy.

Roast Pork Loin and Apple-Orange Chutney

Prep Time: 10 minutes
Cook Time: 20 minutes
Yields: 3 servings

Ingredients **(roast pork loin)**

- 1-2 lb. pork loin
- ½ tsp. salt
- ½ tsp. pepper
- 1 tbsp. butter
- ½ cup apple juice
- 1 small onion (to be sliced into 1-inch pieces)
- Apple / orange chutney (optional)
- Fresh pomegranate seeds (for garnish, optional)

Ingredients **(apple-orange chutney)**

- 4 Granny Smith apples (to be peeled, cored, and cut into 1-inch pieces)
- ½ cup raisins
- ¼ medium white onion (diced)
- 1 tbsp. fresh ginger (minced)
- ½ cup orange juice
- ½ cup apple cider vinegar
- ½ cup brown sugar
- ½ tsp. salt (or to taste)
- 1/8 tsp. red pepper flakes (or to taste)
- 1/8 tsp. ground nutmeg

Instructions **(for the pork loin)**

1. Smear all sides of the pork roast with pepper and salt. Start the Instant Pot on the "Sauté" mode to have the inner pot heated up. When the message "Hot" is displayed, add the butter and allow it to melt. Add the pork roast to the pot. Sear each side for 5 minutes. Add the apple juice and deglaze using a wooden spray to scrape up any brown bit from the pot bottom. Add the onion.
2. Hit the "Cancel" button to turn off the "Sauté" function. Secure the lid and check that the vent valve is on the "Sealing" position. Select the "Pressure Cook" / "Manual" and use the "+/-" button to set the cook time to 20 minutes. When the pot beeps, wait 15 minutes for

natural pressure release. Then shift the valve to "Venting" for a quick release of the remaining pressure. Open the lid, transfer the pork to a cutting board, wait for 5 minutes for it cool a bit. Then slice the pork in ¾-inches and top with chutney and fresh pomegranate seeds (if using).

Instruction (for Apple-Orange Chutney)

1. Combine all the ingredients in the inner pot and give them a good stir. Follow the steps for preparing the pork except that the cook time should be 10 minutes and that the release method after the cooking should be QPR.

2. Open the lid and serve the chutney immediately as hot or allow it to cool.

Beefy Taco Pasta

- **Prep Time:**   10 minutes
- **Cook Time:**   15 minutes
- **Yields:**   2 servings

Ingredients

- ½ tbsp. olive oil
- 1/2 lb. ground beef (95% lean)
- ½ medium yellow onion (to be chopped)
- ½ packet taco seasoning
- 6 ounces campanelle short (chunky twisted) pasta
- 2 tbsps. tomato paste
- ½ large red bell pepper (to be chopped)
- Pinch black pepper
- Salt to taste
- 1 ½ cups water

Instructions

1. Pour the olive oil in the pot and set the cooker on "Sauté." Bring the oil to hot on "NORMAL"/ "MEDIUM" heat. Then add the beef, chopped onions, and ½ tablespoon of the taco seasoning. Then cook. Cut the meat into 1/2-inch chunks as you cook and stir frequently for about 6 minutes or until the onions are tender. Select "Cancel".

2. Add the pasta to the onion and beef mixture and stir to coat. Whisk together the tomato paste, remaining taco seasoning and water in a medium bowl or large measuring cup. Then add the mixture to the pasta in the pot. Stir gently to combine. Set the black peppers on top of the mixture.

3. Lock the lid in place and check to see that the valve is on the "Sealing" position. Select the "Pressure Cook" / "Manual" and cook for 5 minutes on "Low" pressure.
4. Once the pot beeps to show that the time is up, do a quick release of the pressure. Open the lid and gently stir the pasta. Use a rubber spatula to deglaze by scraping any browned bits on the pot's bottom.
5. Add pepper and salt. You can wait a few minutes for the sauce to thicken. You can also serve immediately with cheese.

All-American Pulled Pork

- **Prep Time:**   10 minutes
- **Cook Time:**   60 minutes
- **Yields:**   2 servings

Ingredients

- ½ cup apple cider (unsweetened)
- ½ tbsp. mild smoked paprika
- ½ tbsp. dark brown sugar
- ½ tbsp. standard chili powder
- ¼ tsp. ground mustard (dried)
- ¼ tsp. onion powder
- ¼ tsp. garlic powder
- ¼ tsp. table salt (or to taste)
- ¼ tsp. ground black pepper (or to taste)
- 1 lb. boneless pork shoulder (cut in half and large chunks of fat to be removed)

Instructions

1. Pour the apple cider into the Instant Pot. Combine the smoked paprika, sugar, chili powder, ground mustard, onion powder, pepper, garlic powder, and salt in a small bowl. Pat and smear the mixture all over the pork. Arrange the meat in the pot and lock the lid onto it.
2. If you are cooking on the Max Pressure Cookers, set it to "Pressure Cooker" and cook on maximum pressure for 60 minutes with the "Keep Warm" setting off.
3. If you are cooking on All Pressure Cookers, choose the "Meat" / "Stew" or "Pressure Cook" / "Manual" option and cook on High Pressure for 1 hour 20 minutes with the "Keep Warm" setting off.

4. Another option is the Slow Cook Option. Choose this option and set it on High Pressure for 5 hours with the "Keep Warm" setting off. If it's on, the cook time should not be more than 4 hours.
5. After the cooker beeps at the end of the cook time, wait for 30 minutes for the pressure to be released naturally.
6. Then, unlatch the lid to open the pot. Transfer the pork to a cutting board using a fork and a slotted spoon or a large spatula.
7. Then skim any excess surface fat from the sauce using a flatware tablespoon.
8. Select the "Sauté" option and set it to 10 minutes. Stir a few times as you bring the sauce to a boil. Allow it to cook for about 7 minutes for the sauce to thicken and reduce to about half.
9. Shred the pork with two forks and when the desired consistency is reached, turn off the "Sauté" function. Stir in the shredded pork meat and set the sauce aside for about 4 minutes with the lid on top askew.
10. Once the flavors blend and the meat has absorbed the sauce, stir and serve.

Ground Lamb Kheema

- **Prep Time:**   15 minutes
- **Cook Time:**   45 minutes
- **Yields:**   2 servings

Ingredients

- ½ tbsp. ghee or vegetable oil
- 2 sticks Indian cinnamon (cassia bark, or ¼ regular cinnamon stick, broken into small pieces)
- 2 cardamom pods
- ½ cup chopped yellow onions
- ½ tbsp. minced garlic
- 1 tbsp. minced fresh ginger
- ½ lb. ground lamb
- ½ tsp. garam masala
- ½ tsp. salt (or to taste)
- ¼ tsp. ground turmeric
- ¼ tsp. cayenne pepper (or to taste)
- ½ tsp. ground coriander
- ¼ tsp. ground cumin
- ¼ cup water
- ½ cup frozen peas (to be thawed)

Instructions

1. Start the Instant Pot on the "Sauté" mode. When the "hot" message is displayed, add the ghee and allow it to melt.
2. Add the cinnamon sticks and cardamom pods and wait for about 10 seconds to let them sizzle.
3. Add the onion, garlic, and ginger and keep stirring from time to time as it cooks for about 1 or 2 minutes.
4. Add the lamb and stir until the clumps break up as it cooks for about 2 or 3 minutes.
5. Add the garam masala, cayenne, turmeric, coriander, cumin, salt, and water.
6. Cancel sautéing and secure the lid into place. Ensure that the pressure release valve is on the "Sealing" position. Set to "Manual" / "Pressure Cook" and the pressure to "High" with the time to 10 minutes.
7. When the cooking ends, wait for 10 minutes of natural pressure release and allow the manual release of the remaining pressure.
8. Stir in the peas and cover for about 5 minutes for the peas to be heated through. Then serve.

Braised Beef Shank

- **Prep Time:**   15 minutes
- **Cook Time:**   35 minutes
- **Yields:**   2 servings

Ingredients
- 1 - 1 ½ lbs. beef shank
Ingredients (for the Marinade)
- 1 tsp. peppercorns
- 1/3 tsp. salt
- 1/3 tsp. sugar
- 1 tbsp. soy sauce (light)
Ingredients (for the Sauce)
- 1 tsp. salt (or to taste)
- 1 tsp. sugar (or to taste)
- ¼ cup soy sauce (light)
- 1 tbsp. soy sauce (dark)
- 1 clover
- 1 anise
- ½ tsp. cumin

- 1 bay leaf
- 1 tbsp. Jasmine green tea
- 1 tsp. sesame oil
- ¼ tsp. ginger (fresh and shredded)
- 1 green onion (to be chopped)
- 2 cups water

Instructions

1. Add the marinade ingredients to the beef shank in a tightly sealed ziplock bag or another airtight food container. Shake it well and refrigerate for one day.
2. Pour the rinsed peppercorns in the Instant Pot and add the beef shank with all ingredients. Stir well for everything to combine.
3. Close the lid tightly and make sure the pressure release valve is on the "Sealing" position. Press the "Pressure Cook" o/"Manual" button and use the "+/--" button to set the cooking time to 35 minutes.
4. When the cooking is done, allow 10 minutes of natural pressure release and do a quick release of the remaining pressure.
5. Transfer the cooked beef shank into a clean container and chill for 4 hours. Slice and then serve.

Pork Vindaloo - Pork Ribs in Spicy Garlic Chili Sauce

- **Prep Time:**   10 minutes
- **Cook Time:**   35 minutes
- **Yields:**   2-3 servings

Ingredients

- ½ tbsp. salt (or to taste)
- ¾ lb. baby back ribs
- 1 whole dried red chili
- ½ tbsp. cumin seeds
- 1 whole clove
- ½ cinnamon stick
- 1 tbsp. Kashmiri red chili powder
- ½ tsp. ground turmeric
- 1 ½ tbsps. oil
- ½ cup red onion (minced)
- 1 ½ tbsps. garlic (minced)
- ½ tbsp. ginger (minced)
- ½ cup red wine vinegar

- ¼ cup chicken broth (low-sodium; or vegetable broth)
- 1 ½ tbsps. brown sugar
- Chopped green onions (for garnish)
- Crushed red pepper (for garnish)

Instructions

1. Cut the ribs into a smaller size, if needed to fit in the Instant Pot, and sprinkle salt all over. Set aside.
2. In a spice mill or coffee grinder, combine the chili, cumin seeds, clove, cinnamon stick, Kashmiri chili powder, and turmeric and grind all to powder.
3. Press the "Sauté" button on the Instant Pot and pour the oil to heat for about 1 minute. Then add the onion, garlic, and ginger. Let them sauté for about 2 minutes. Stir in the powdered spice mixture and vinegar. Add the pork rib and stir while cooking and have the ribs coated. The mixture should turn to a rich reddish-brown in about 3 minutes. Then add the broth and brown sugar. Stir well and bring to a simmer.
4. Press "Cancel" to stop sautéing. Close the lid in place and set the vent valve to the "Sealing" position. Select "Meat" / "Stew" option and set the time for 25 minutes.
5. Once the pot beeps, allow 10 minutes of NPR and use the QR to allow the remaining pressure out.
6. Open the lid and select the "Sauté" mode again so that the sauce can simmer and thicken while draining off the excess fat.
7. Garnish with crushed peppers and green onions and serve on anything meal.

Mediterranean Lamb Shanks

- **Prep Time:**   30 minutes
- **Cook Time:**   90 minutes
- **Yields:**   2 servings

Ingredients (for Marinade Mixture)

- ¼ cup olive oil
- 1 ½ cloves garlic (minced)
- 1 tbsp. brown sugar
- ½ tbsp. each dried oregano, smoked paprika, and kosher salt
- ¼ tsp. cumin
- ½ cinnamon stick

Ingredients (for Lamb Shanks)

- ¾ - 1 lb. lamb shanks (preferably skinless, about 1 or 2 shanks)
- 1/8 cup olive oil
- ½ onion (to be chopped)

- 1 ½ carrot (to be chopped)
- 1 bay leaf
- 1 cup red wine
- 2 cups beef broth (warmed)
- 1 ½ tbsps. cornstarch
- 1 ½ tbsps. cold water
- ¼ cup chopped Italian parsley (for garnish, optional)

Instructions

1. Mix all ingredients of marinade mixture in a medium bowl and add the lamb shanks to be well coated with the mixture. Leave for at least 30 minutes to marinate.
2. After marinating, add the olive oil to the Instant Pot and select the "Sauté" function. When the oil gets hot, brown the meat for about 3 minutes per side until all sides are brown. If you're having a small size and the pot will be crowded, cook in batches. Have the browned meat transferred into a shallow dish and cover with foil. Then add onion, bay leaf, carrots, and the remaining marinade to the IP and keep sautéing until the chopped onion are soft, usually about 5 minutes.
3. Pour the wine to the pot. To deglaze, use a wooden spoon to scrape the brown bits from the pot bottom. Allow the sauce to simmer for 10 minutes until it reduces to half. Then add the broth and transfer the meat back into the pot. Turn it once to coat.
4. Select "Cancel" to turn off the pot. Have lid well secured and the vent closed. From the display panel select "Manual" / "Pressure Cook" function and program the pot to cook for 30 minutes using the "+/-" keys. Then allow 15 minutes of the natural pressure release and do a quick release of the remaining pressure. Carefully transfer the meat into a shallow dish and cover with foil. The juice should be reserved.
5. Strain the liquid to get rid of the solid and return it to the pot. Then mix cornstarch and cold water in a small bowl. Stir the mixture into the pot until thickened while the program is returned to "Sauté".
6. Top with gravy and serve alongside your favorite. Garnish with the parsley, if using.

Brisket Skewers

- **Prep Time:**   10 minutes
- **Cook Time:**   50 minutes
- **Yields:**   2-3 servings

Ingredients

- 1 lb. flat- or first-cut lean brisket (cut into 1 ½-inch cube)
- ½ tbsp. mild paprika (smoked)
- ½ tsp. onion powder
- ¼ tsp. garlic powder

- ¼ tsp. table salt (or to taste)
- 6-8 bamboo or metal skewers (4-inch)
- ½ cup water
- 2 oz. liquid smoke (½ bottle)

Instructions

1. Add the first 5 ingredients listed, up till and including table salt, in a medium bowl. Toss until the meat is thoroughly and evenly coated.
2. Thread 2 cubes through each skewer.
3. Combine the water and liquid smoke in the Instant Pot. Put a pressure cooker-safe trivet into the cooker and arrange the skewers onto the trivet.
4. Lock the lid in place and select "Pressure Cook" on Max for 42 minutes with the "Keep Warm" setting off, if you're using Max Pressure Cooker.
5. If you're using All Pressure Cooker, choose option "Meat" / "Stew" or "Pressure Cook" / "manual". Cook on High Pressure with the time set for 50 minutes and the "Keep Warm" setting off.
6. After the cook time is up, wait 20 minutes for the natural release of pressure. Unlatch to open the pot.
7. Heat a grill pan (cast-iron) over medium-high heat. Once it starts smoking, set the skewers on the grill pan and grill for 2 minutes or until it's crisp and browned. Turn it occasionally.
8. You can grill for high heat if you choose to cook directly over the heat source by simply brushing the grill grates and preparing.

Balsamic Apple Pork Tenderloin

- **Prep Time:**   5 minutes
- **Cook Time:**   35 minutes
- **Yields:**   2 servings

Ingredients
- ½ sprig rosemary
- 1 ½ sprigs thyme fresh
- Kitchen twine
- ½ tbsp. canola oil
- ¾ lb. pork tenderloin (not loin roast)
- ½ small onion (finely chopped)
- 1 clove garlic (minced)
- 1 ¼ tbsps. balsamic vinegar
- ¼ cup chicken broth
- ½ apple (peeled and chopped)

- ¼ tsp. kosher salt (or to taste)
- 1 tbsp. honey
- ½ tbsp. butter
- 1 ¼ tsps. cornstarch
- Fresh thyme (for garnish, optional)
- Pomegranate seeds (for garnish, optional)

Instructions

1. Wrap a few loops of kitchen twine around rosemary and thyme and tie firmly.
2. Start the Instant Pot on the "Sauté" function and add oil when it's hot. Add meat to the oil when hot and brown each side 3-4 minutes. Don't worry about cooking as it will not cook through at this point. Once the meat turns brown, transfer it to a plate and cover loosely using foil.
3. Add onion while the pot is still on the "Sauté" mode. After 3 minutes or when the onion is soft, add garlic and cook for about 2 minutes more. But if the onion is too dry, you may add a bit of broth. Add balsamic vinegar. Deglaze the pot by using a wooden spoon to scrape the brown bit off the bottom of the pot.
4. Add (more) broth, apple, and salt and stir well to combine. Then add the herb bundle and stir well to mix. Add the pork tenderloin and nestle in the sauce. Turn it once to coat.
5. Tightly secure the lid, and ensure that the vent is closed. Press the "Pressure Cook" / "Manual" button and set it to cook on Low Pressure. Set the cook time to 20 minutes using the "+/-" button. When the cooking is done, select "Cancel" and wait for 15 minutes for natural pressure release. Then do the quick release of the remaining pressure.
6. Open the pot and check the temperature of the meat core using a meat thermometer. You will cook again if it's less than 137 degrees F. Then, carefully transfer the pork from the cooker to a cutting board. Cover it loosely with foil. Return the IP to the "Sauté" mode and add butter and honey. Stir well to mix. Cook by stirring occasionally for 5 minutes. If the meat didn't reach 137 degrees, turn it into the pot now and continue cooking until the desired temperature is reached.
7. Take the herb bundle out of the pot. Also, scoop out 1/3 of the liquid and whisk in the cornstarch in a small bowl. Add the mixture back to the apple mixture. Stir well to thicken.
8. Slice the pork tenderloin to form medallions. Serve with topped the balsamic-apple mixture. If using, serve with thyme and pomegranate seeds.

Irish Lamb Stew

- **Prep Time:**   5 minutes
- **Cook Time:**   25 minutes
- **Yields:**   2-3 servings

Ingredients

- 1 tbsp. olive oil
- ½ lb. lamb stew meat (cut into ¾-inch cubes)
- ½ onion (to be finely diced)
- 1 tbsp. flour
- 1 cup chicken (or beef broth, warmed)
- ½ lb. russet potatoes (to be peeled and cut into ½-inch dices)
- 1 carrot (to be cut into ½-inch dices)
- 4 oz. Guinness (or other dark beer)
- 1 tbsp. tomato paste
- 1 tsp. salt (or to taste)
- ½ tsp. Dijon
- ½ tsp. dried thyme
- ½ tsp. dried rosemary
- ¼ tsp. pepper
- Flat-leaf parsley (for garnish, optional)
- Fresh ground pepper (for garnish, optional)

Instructions

1. Start the Instant Pot on the "Sauté" function and add the olive oil to the hot pot.
2. Add the meat when the oil is hot and brown each side for 3 – 4 minutes.
3. Add broth to the pot, then deglaze by scraping the brown bits off the bottom of the pot, using a wooden spoon.
4. Add the remaining ingredients. Stir well to combine.
5. Select "Cancel" to turn off the pot. Secure the lid and check to be sure that the vent valve is on the "Sealing" position.
6. On the display panel, select "Manual" / "Pressure Cook" function and program the cook time to 15 minutes, using the "+/-" keys.
7. When the pot beeps at the end of cook time, allow 10 minutes of natural pressure release and do the quick release of the remaining pressure.

Chunky Beef Chili

- **Prep Time:**   5 minutes
- **Cook Time:**   22 minutes
- **Yields:**   2 servings

Ingredients

- ¾ lb. beef stew meat (to be cut into 1-inch to 1 1/2-inch piece)
- 1 tbsp. vegetable oil (divided)
- 1 small onion be (to be chopped)

- 1 small Jalapeno pepper (to be minced)
- 15 oz. tomatoes with chilies (to be diced)
- Very small water

Instructions

1. Selecting the "Sauté" function on the Instant Pot and add the vegetable oil. Brown stew meat on all sides. You may season with salt if you like.
2. Add the chopped onion, sliced jalapeno pepper, and diced tomatoes.
3. Secure the lid in place and choose the "Beef"/"Stew" setting or "Pressure Cook" / "Manual" with the time set to 22 minutes.
4. When the timer beeps, do the quick release of pressure. Then remove the lid carefully.
5. Top with shredded cheese, sour cream, or any other topping of your choice while serving.

Vortex Plus - Honey Sriracha Pork Tenderloin

- **Prep Time:**   20 minutes
- **Cook Time:**   25 minutes
- **Yields:**   2 servings

Ingredients

- 1- 1 ½ lbs. pork tenderloin
- 2 tbsps. honey
- 2 tbsps. sriracha hot sauce (or to taste)
- 1 ½ tsps. kosher salt (or to taste)

Instructions

1. Make a hole in the center of the pork tenderloin using a pointed metal skewer. Then insert the spit. Thread the rotisserie fork through from each side. Tighten the screws and hold the port firmly in place.
2. Mix the honey, sriracha, and salt in a small bowl and brush over the pork tenderloin evenly.
3. Station the drip pan at the cooking chamber bottom.
4. Select "Airfry" on the display panel with the temperature adjusted to 350°F and time 20 minutes. Then press "Start."
5. When the message "Add Food" displays, lift the spit into the cooking chamber using the rotisserie fetch tool. Secure the ends of the spit with the red rotisserie release lever.
6. Close the door and press "Rotate".
7. Serve when the rotation stops.

Savory Mole Pork Tacos

- **Prep Time:**   5 minutes
- **Cook Time:**   75 minutes
- **Yields:**   2 servings

Ingredients (for Savory Mole Pork Tacos)

- 1 cup fresh salsa
- 1 tbsp. chili powder
- 1tbsp. dried oregano
- 1tbsp. unsweetened cocoa powder
- ½ tbsp. kosher salt (or to taste)
- 1 lb. boneless pork butt (or shoulder, cut into 3 pieces)
- ¼ cup beef broth
- ½ onion (quartered)

Ingredients (for serving)

- Corn tortillas (warmed)
- Cilantro (chopped)
- Sour cream
- Additional salsa
- Lime wedges

Instructions

1. Add all ingredients except the onion and broth in a medium bowl.
2. Pour the beef broth into the Instant Pot. Add quartered onions
3. Evenly layer the pork pieces on top of the onions.
4. Add any additional marinade to the pork pieces but don't stir.
5. Tightly secure the lid, ensuring that the valve is on the "Sealing" position. Then select the "Manual" / "Pressure Cook" function on the display panel and us the "+/-" to program the cook time to 60 minutes.
6. When the time is up, allow the natural pressure release for 10 minutes and thereafter do a quick release of the remaining pressure.
7. Open the lid and transfer the meat from the pot to a cutting board to shred.
8. After shredding the meat, return to the pot and stir to mix with the mixture.
9. Serve on warm tortillas and cilantro, sour cream, salsa, and lime wedges.

CHAPTER 5: THE INSTANT POT POULTRY AND CHICKEN RECIPES FOR BEGINNERS

One of the best recipes you can bring together in the Instant Pot is the class poultry foods. There's virtually no meal you can't try with chickens. Turkey distinguishes itself as a poultry meal that comes out well with the support from seasonings, herbs, and spices when they all meet in the Instant pot. Breasts, thighs, meatballs, stuffing, and the rest all come together to show how great poultry meals can be. While chicken and turkey readily come to mind when discussing poultry meal, it should also be noted that the egg also is from poultry. Here are a few examples of recipes from poultry.

Chicken Fajitas

- **Prep Time:**   5 minutes
- **Cook Time:**   40 minutes
- **Yields:**   2-3 servings

Ingredients

- 1 small onion (to be peeled, halved, and sliced into thin half-moons)
- ¼ cup chicken broth
- 4 oz. fajita seasoning (there's a gluten-free version)
- 1 tbsp. pickled jalapeño rings (with some pickling juice)
- 1 lb. frozen chicken tenders
- ½ lb. frozen bell pepper strips

Instructions

1. Combine the onion, broth, half of the fajita seasoning, and all the jalapeno rings in the Instant Pot and stir well. Place Instant Pot's rack in the mixture let its handles be upward. (You may use an open vegetable steamer instead)
2. Arrange half of the chicken tenders on the rack and sprinkle with the half other the remaining fajita seasoning (that is a quarter of the whole volume). Top with the remaining tenders. Sprinkle them with the remaining fajita seasoning. Then top with the bell pepper without stirring.
3. Lock the lid in place and press the "Pressure Cook" and cook on Max Pressure with the time set for 12 minutes and the "Keep Warm" off. That is if you're cooking on Max Pressure Cooker.

4. If you're cooking on All Pressure Cooker, select "Poultry" and "Pressure Cook" or "Manual". Cook on High Pressure for 15 minutes and have the "Keep Warm" setting off.

5. When the cook time is up, do the quick release of pressure by shifting the valve to "Venting". Using silicone cooking mitts or thick hot pad, remove the rack (or steamer) from the pot (you can use kitchen tongs). Allow the chicken to fall into the sauce below and stir well.

6. Then press the "Sauté" button and set it for "High" "More" or "Custom 400°F" with the time set for 15 minutes.

7. Bring the sauce to a simmer as you use a slotted spoon to transfer the chicken from the pot into a serving platter together with the vegetables. Let the sauce boil while stirring frequently until it reduces to a glaze, about 8 minutes.

8. Turn off the "Sauté" function by pressing the "Cancel" button. Pour the sauce on the chicken and vegetables and then serve.

Turkey Breast

- **Prep Time:**   10 minutes
- **Cook Time:**   40 minutes
- **Yields:**   2-3 servings

Ingredients

- 2 lb. bone-in turkey breast
- 1 tbsp. butter (softened)
- ¼ tsp. paprika
- ¼. Tsp. garlic powder
- ¼ tsp. salt (or to taste)
- ½ cup chicken broth or water
- ¼ medium onion
- 1 small celery stalks (cut in half)
- ½ tbsp. cornstarch (plus additional ½ tsp.)

Instructions

1. Allow the turkey breast to thaw in the fridge for 3 days if frozen, leaving it in its default wrapping. Rinse and wash away any gravy mix or giblets off the cavity. Allow it to drain in a colander and pat dry with paper towels. Open the skin on top of the breast using a knife and your fingers but don't cut it off.

2. In a small bowl, combine the butter, herb seasonings, and salt. Spread some of the mixture under the skin and the turkey breast using fingertips. Carefully lay the skin back on the mixture. Then spread the remaining mixture on top of it.
3. Pour the chicken broth or water in the Instant Pot with the trivet inside.
4. Arrange the remaining onion and celery under the breast if it has a cavity. If not, place them on the trivet and arrange the turkey breasts there with the sides up.
5. Tightly lock in the lid with the vent valve set to the "Sealing" position. Select "Pressure Cook" / "Manual" and use the "+/-" button to set the time to 32 minutes and cook on High Pressure. Wait for about 13 to 20 minutes for it to come to pressure.
6. When the pot beeps to signal the end of cook time, allow the natural pressure release for 20 minutes and do a manual release of the remaining pressure by turning the valve to "Venting" for the floating valve to drop.
7. Open and use two large metal spatulas or spoons (not forks as they will release all the juices inside the turkey) to transfer the turkey to a baking sheet lined with foil. Meanwhile, preheat broiler. Broil until the skin is golden brown, usually about 3- 5 minutes.
8. Pour about ½ cup of drippings in the Instant Pot pan and do whatever you like with the rest of the liquid. Mix about 1 tablespoon of custard with cornstarch and pour in the turkey drippings.
9. Press the "Sauté" button and allow the gravy to cook for about 8 minutes while stirring occasionally for it to slightly thicken.

Chicken Cordon Bleu

- **Prep Time:**   15 minutes
- **Cook Time:**   15 minutes
- **Yields:**   2 servings

Ingredients

- ¼ cup chicken broth
- 1 lb. chicken breasts (about 2 chicken breasts)
- ½ tbsp. butter (to be melted)
- 1 oz. thinly sliced ham
- 1 oz. Swiss (or provolone) cheese
- Kosher salt (to taste)
- Pepper (to taste)
- ½ tbsp. olive oil
- ½ tbsp butter (cold)
- ½ cup panko bread crumbs

- 1 tbsp. Dijon mustard
- 1 tbsp. heavy cream
- Snipped chives (as desired, for garnish)

Instructions

1. Pour chicken broth into your pot.
2. Arrange the chicken breasts (smooth side down), between two sheets of plastic wrap. Pout it to ¼-inch thickness.
3. Have the melted butter brushed evenly over the breasts. Add ham and cheese. Then sprinkle with salt and pepper to taste.
4. Roll up each breast beginning from one of the short ends. Arrange each chicken bundle in the Instant Pot, seam side down.
5. Tightly secure the lid, ensuring that the vent is closed. Select the "Manual" / "Pressure Cook" function and use the "+/-" keys to program the pot for 5 minutes.
6. When the cook time is up, allow the natural release of pressure for another 5 minutes and thereafter do a quick release of the remaining pressure.
7. Meanwhile, heat the cold butter and olive oil in a nonstick skillet. Add panko 1/8 tablespoon of salt and some grinds of pepper.
8. Keep stirring as you cook. When the crumbs turn golden brown, remove from the heat and continue stirring for 30 seconds to avoid burning.
9. Now combine Dijon and cream in a small bowl and set aside.
10. After the cooking, carefully transfer the roll-ups from the pot to the skillet, dipping them to coat the bottom with crumbs. Place on two serving plates.
11. Sprinkle the top of the roll-ups with the remaining toasted crumbs, drizzle with Dijon and garnish with snipped chives.

Salsa Chicken

- **Prep Time:**   5 minutes
- **Cook Time:**   15 minutes
- **Yields:**   2 servings

Ingredients

- 2 chicken breasts (fresh or frozen)
- ½ jar salsa
- ¼ cup water (or chicken broth)
- ½ cup Greek yogurt (plain fat-free)

Instructions

1. Set chicken breasts to the Instant Pot inner pot.
2. Pour the chicken broth or water.
3. Add salsa as a topping.
4. Select "Manual" / "Poultry" / "Pressure Cook" and set on High for 15 minutes.
5. When time is up with the beep signal, wait for the natural pressure release for 10 minutes and quick release the remaining pressure.
6. Allow it to simmer on the "Sauté" mode for 5 minutes or less, depending on how thick you want the sauce to be.
7. Turn off the sauté function and wait for 10 minutes for the sauce to cool.
8. Transfer the chicken to a plate and chop with a knife. You may also shred it with a fork and return it to the pot.
9. Add in the yogurt and stir.
10. Serve over rice, taco salad, or tortillas

Creamy White Chicken Chili

- **Prep Time:**   5 minutes
- **Cook Time:**   35 minutes
- **Yields:**   2-3 servings

Ingredients
- ½ tsp. olive oil
- ½ onion (to be finely diced)
- ½ garlic cloves (to be minced)
- ½ cups chicken broth
- 1 lb. chicken thighs (boneless, skinless)
- 10 oz. cannellini beans (or 7 oz. drained and rinsed beans, or other canned white beans)
- 3 oz. canned chopped green chili
- ½ tbsp. chili powder
- ½ tbsp. cumin
- ½ tsp. kosher salt (or to taste)
- ¼ tsp. black pepper (or to taste)
- ¼ cup butter
- 2 tbsp. flour
- ½ cup milk (to be warmed)
- ¼ cup sour cream
- ½ tbsp. lime juice
- Chopped cilantro (for garnish, optional)
- Shredded Monterey jack cheese (for garnish, optional)

Instructions

1. Start the Instant Pot on the "Sauté" function and add the olive oil when hot.
2. Add the onion to the oil when hot and sauté for 3 to 4 minutes, until soft. Add garlic and continue sautéing for 1 – 2 minutes more.
3. Deglaze by adding broth to the pot and use a wooden spatula to scrape the brown bits off from the pot's bottom.
4. Add the chicken with beans, chilies, chili powder, pepper, and salt. Stir all well to combine.
5. Stop sautéing by pressing "Cancel". Then tightly secure the lid with the vent valve on the "Sealing" position. Select the "Manual" / "Pressure Cook" function on the display panel and use the "+/-" keys to set the time for 15 minutes.
6. When the cook time is up, allow natural pressure release for minutes and do the quick release of the remaining pressure.
7. Carefully transfer the chicken to a cutting board and shred. Return it to the pot. Melt the butter in a medium bowl and whisk in the flour to combine. Stir the mixture into the pot and simmer for about 2 minutes until thickened. Revert to "Sauté" mode when needed. Then stir in the milk, lime juice, and sour cream. Adjust seasonings as needed.
8. Serve hot with cilantro and shredded cheese as a topping, if using.

Chinese Tea Eggs (Marbled Eggs)

- **Prep Time:**   4 minutes
- **Cook Time:**   4 minutes
- **Passive Time:**   18 hours
- **Yields:**   2 servings

Ingredients

- 2 eggs
- Water enough to cover the eggs
- ¼ cup soy sauce
- ¼ tsp. sugar
- star anise
- 1 bag black tea
- ½ cinnamon stick
- Peel from an orange

Instructions

1. Set the steam rack in the inner pot and place the eggs.

2. Cover the eggs with water and tea bag, star anise, soy sauce, cinnamon stick, and sugar.
3. Stir all together to combine.
4. Add the orange peel.
5. Secure the lid tightly and shift the steam release valve to the "Sealing position."
6. Select "Pressure Cook" / "Manual" and set to High pressure. Use the "+/-" keys to program the cook time to 4 minutes.
7. Once the pot beeps for time up, do the quick release of pressure.
8. Using a teaspoon, crack the eggs all over but leave the shells on. (It will form a marble-like design.)
9. Return all the eggs into the Instant Pot close the lid on for 18 hours or, at least, overnight. (The longer you leave it, the stronger and saltier flavor you get.)
10. Then run your eggs under cold water and take out the shells.
11. Eat immediately or refrigerate for up to a week.

Turkey Breast and Mashed Potatoes

- **Prep Time:**   10 minutes
- **Cook Time:**   45 minutes
- **Yields:**   2 servings

Ingredients (Turkey Breast and Mashed Potatoes)
- 1 ½ lb. fresh turkey breast
- ½ tbsp. oil
- ¼ tsp. ground sage
- ½ tsp. dried basil
- ¼ tsp. dried tarragon
- ¼ tsp. thyme (or any other herb seasoning)
- ½ tsp. salt (or to taste)
- ¼ tsp. pepper
- ¾ cup turkey (or chicken) broth or water
- 1 carrot (to be cut into 2-inch pieces)
- 1 stalk celery (to be cut into 2-inch pieces)
- ½ small onion (to be cut into 4 pieces)
- 1 to 2 russet potatoes (to be peeled, quartered)

Ingredients (for Gravy)
- 1 ¼ tbsp. butter (or oil)
- 1 tbsp. flour

Instructions

1. Wash the turkey and pat dry. Combine the oil, herbs, pepper, and salt to make a paste. Rub the paste all over the turkey breast.
2. Cut and toss the vegetables (except potatoes) and apple into the IP. Add the broth or water. Position the trivet over the mixture and set the turkey breast on it.
3. You can add potatoes now or wait till after the turkey is done as it will boil in just 4-6 minutes. If you're adding the potatoes now, use a tin foil to hold them and fit them anywhere in the pot.
4. Close the lid securely vent closed. Hit the "Pressure Cook" / "Manual" button and use the "+/-" button to set the time to 24 minutes. Once the pot beeps, allow 15 minutes of natural pressure release. Meanwhile, turn the broiler on the baking sheet lined with tin foil.
5. Do a quick release of the remaining pressure for the pin to drop. Transfer the breast to the baking sheet to brown in the broiler for about 3-5 minutes or less. Meanwhile, mash the potatoes and add butter, milk, cream, pepper, and salt.
6. The breast should have browned by now. Begin to prepare the gravy by straining the cooking liquid and do away with the veggies. Start the Instant Pot on the "Sauté" mode and add butter or oil into the pot. Stir in the flour and whisk for a minute. Add all the strained liquid all at once. Whisk thoroughly as you bring to boil and it thickens. Add pepper and salt to taste.
7. Serve and enjoy.

Jerk Chicken and Cornbread

- **Prep Time:**   5 minutes
- **Cook Time:**   30 minutes
- **Yields:**   2 servings

Ingredients (for Chicken and Cornbread)
- 4 ½ oz. corn muffin mix (to be prepared according to package instructions)
- 1 tbsp. thinly sliced scallions
- ½ jalapeno (to be seeded and minced)
- ½ tbsp. olive oil
- ¼ cup chicken broth
- 1 lb. chicken thighs (skinless)
- Lime wedges plus additional sliced scallions (for garnish, optional)

Ingredients (for Jerk Mixture)
- 1 tbsp. molasses
- 1 tbsp. lime juice
- 1 tbsp. paprika
- 1 tbsp. olive oil
- 1 tbsp. garlic powder

- 1 tsp. allspice
- ½ tsp. ground nutmeg
- ½ tsp. kosher salt (or to taste)
- ½ tsp. cayenne (or to taste)
- ¼ tsp. pepper (or to taste)

Instructions
1. Stir in the scallions and jalapeno into the corn muffin mix being prepared according to the package directions. Using nonstick spray, coat the inside of silicone egg bite molds and divide the corn muffin mixture into the molds. Tap on the counter so as to even the batter and release, bubbles. Then loosely cover with foil but don't seal.
2. Add the jerk mixture ingredients in a medium bowl and stir until well combined. Set aside half of the jerk mixture. Pour the olive oil into the Instant Pot and sauté until hot.
3. Meanwhile, pour the remaining jerk mixture onto the chicken thigh to coat. Brown each side of the chicken 3 to 4 minutes. Don't worry if the meat is not cooked through this time. You may do this in batches if the pot will be crowded. When the meat is brown, transfer it to a shallow dish and have it covered loosely with foil.
4. Add the broth into the IP. Deglaze by scraping the brown bits from the bottom using a wooden spoon. Then evenly layer the chicken on the pot and spread the remaining jerk mixture on it.
5. Insert the steam rack or trivet and use a foil sling to set the egg bite mold onto the riser. Then, turn off the pot by pressing the "Cancel" button. Tightly secure the lid, ensuring that the vent is closed. Then select the "Manual" / "Pressure Cook" function and set the time for 10 minutes, using the "+/-" keys.
6. Wait 5 minutes for the natural release of pressure after the pot beeps and do a quick release of the remaining pressure.
7. Serve with cornbread and garnish with lime wedges and additional scallions. (optional).

Apricot Pineapple Chicken Thighs

- **Prep Time:**   10 minutes
- **Cook Time:**   30 minutes
- **Yields:**   2 servings

Ingredients
- 1 tbsp. vegetable oil
- 2 chicken thighs (skin and visible fat removed)
- ¼ cup apricot-pineapple jam
- 1 tbsp. soy sauce
- ½ cup water

Instructions

1. Start the Instant Pot on "Sauté" and set to "High". After heating for a few minutes, add oil to the pot followed by chicken thighs. Allow them to cook until golden brown, for about 3 minutes. Then cancel sautéing.
2. Whisk together the jam and soy sauce in a medium bowl and toss in the thighs until well coated.
3. Position the wire trivet inside the pot and pour water. Set the thighs on the trivet and press "Cancel" on the display panel.
4. Cover the pot with the lid and latch. Select "Pressure Cook" / "Manual" and cook on High Pressure for 20 minutes.
5. When the pot beeps, allow 10 minutes of natural release of pressure and thereafter do the quick release of the remaining pressure.
6. Transfer the thighs into a serving plate and press "Cancel". Bring the liquid to a simmer with the pot set to "High Sauté". Whisk frequently for 5 minutes. Serve the chicken with the drizzle of the thickened sauce.

Arroz con Pollo (Chicken with Rice)

- **Prep Time:**   10 minutes
- **Cook Time:**   30 minutes
- **Yields:**   2 servings

Ingredients

- ½ tbsp. California chili powder
- ½ tsp. ground cumin
- ½ tsp. crushed dried Mexican oregano
- ½ tsp. coarse salt (plus more for seasoning)
- ¼ tsp. freshly ground black pepper
- ¼ tsp. onion powder
- ¼ tsp. garlic powder
- 3 boneless chicken thighs
- 1 ½ tbsp. vegetable oil (divided)
- ½ cup long-grain (or jasmine rice)
- ¼ medium white onion (to be finely chopped)
- 1 garlic cloves (to be minced)
- 2 Roma tomatoes (to be finely chopped)
- ½ cup chicken broth
- 4 oz. tomato sauce
- 2 cilantro sprigs
- Pico de Gallo Verde (for garnish, optional)
- Pimiento-stuffed olives (sliced, for garnish, optional)

Instructions

1. Combine the chili powder, ground cumin, oregano, onion powder, garlic powder, pepper, and salt in a small bowl. Mix thoroughly and sprinkle over the chicken thighs.
2. Start the Instant Pot on the "Sauté" mode and set to "More" or "High".
3. Add 1 tablespoon of vegetable oil in the pot. When hot, add the chicken tight and brown each side by frying for 5 – 7 minutes. Remove the chicken and place it on a heat-resistant plate.
4. Heat the remaining ½ tablespoon of vegetable oil in the Instant Pot. Add the rice to sauté until it turns golden brown. Add the garlic and onion and continue sautéing for 2 or 3 minutes more or until the onion is translucent. Then stir in the tomatoes.
5. Add the chicken broth and also the tomato sauce. Season with salt as desired and return the chicken to the pot. Add the cilantro as a topping.
6. Tightly secure the lid and ensure that the release valve is on the "Sealing" position. Select "Manual" / "Pressure Cook" and cook on High Pressure with the timer set to 12 minutes.
7. When the cook time is up, do a natural release of pressure for 9 minutes and shift the valve to "Venting" for the remaining pressure to be released. Then unlock and uncover the pot.
8. Serve immediately without the cilantro. Garnish with Pico-del Gallo Verde.

Turkey and Stuffing

- **Prep Time:**   5 minutes
- **Cook Time:**   30 minutes
- **Yields:**   2 servings

Ingredients

- 1 lb. turkey breast (fresh)
- ½ tsp. salt (or to taste)
- ½ tsp. pepper (or to taste)
- ¼ cup chicken broth
- 3 oz. stuffing mix
- 6 oz. cream of chicken soup
- 4 oz. sour cream plain Greek yogurt (or mayonnaise)
- 1 cup frozen green beans

Instructions

1. Cut the turkey breast into 2-4 cuts of not more than 1-inch thick. Season with pepper and salt.

2. Layer the turkey evenly in the pot and add the broth. Secure the lid in place with the vent closed.
3. Select "Manual" / "Pressure Cook" on the display panel and program to cook for 7 minutes. In the meantime, carefully fold together in a medium bowl the stuffing mix, chicken soup cream, and sour cream and slightly combine. Don't mix too much.
4. Once the Instant Pot beeps when the time is up, do the quick release of the pressure. If the turkey is not fully cooked, add 2 tablespoons of water and tightly seal again. Proceed with the "Manual" / "Pressure Cook" option but this time for 2 minutes after which you'll quick-release.
5. Evenly layer the frozen beans on the turkey without stirring. Start again the "Manual" / "Pressure Cook" option with the time set to 2 minutes. Then do the quick release of the pressure when the time is up.
6. Arrange the stuffing mixture in an even layer on the beans without stirring. One more time, start again the "Manual" / "Pressure Cook" option with the time set to 4 minutes. Then do the quick release of the pressure.
7. Stuffing may have absorbed all the liquid. So the seal may not be complete during this process. Don't worry!
8. Serve hot and side with cranberry sauce.

Turkey Meatballs with Buttery Rice Pilaf

- **Prep Time:**   5 minutes
- **Cook Time:**   40 minutes
- **Yields:**   2 servings

Ingredients
- 1 ¼ cups chicken broth
- ½ cup raw white basmati rice (plus 1 tbsp.)
- ¼ cup frozen chopped onion (or 1 small yellow or white onion; to be peeled and chopped)
- 1 tsp. fresh sage leaves (stemmed and minced, or ½ tsp. dried sage)
- ½ tsp. stemmed fresh thyme leaves (or ¼ tsp. dried thyme)
- ¼ tsp. table salt (or to taste)
- 1 lb. frozen mini (or bite-sized turkey meatballs)
- 1 tbsp. butter

Instructions

1. Start the Instant Pot on the "Sauté" mode and set to "High", "More" or "Custom 400°F" with the timer set for 10 minutes.
2. Add the broth to the pot and the next five ingredients after the rice. Keep stirring until many wisps of appear on the liquid.

3. Add the meatballs and stir.
4. Turn off the "Sauté" function by pressing the "Cancel" button. Add the butter to the pot and lock the lid into the place.
5. The first option is to use Max Pressure Cooker; select Pressure Cook on for 10 minutes and have the "Keep Warm" setting off.
6. Another option is the All Pressure Cooker; using this, select "Poultry" / "Pressure Cook" or "Manual" and cook on High pressure for 12 minutes. Let the "Keep Warm" setting be off.
7. Once the pot beeps when the time is up, turn the valve to "Venting" for the manual release of pressure. When the pressure has been brought down, unlatch the lid to open the pot.
8. Stir well and serve. Enjoy!

Chicken With Leeks and Mushrooms

- **Prep Time:**   15 minutes
- **Cook Time:**   10 minutes
- **Yields:**   2-3 servings

Ingredients

- 3 chicken breasts (boneless and skinless)
- ¼ tsp. Pink Himalayan salt (or to taste, or Celtic Salt)
- ¼ tsp. pepper (or to taste)
- 2 tbsps. butter (or ghee)
- 1 ½ lbs. leeks (white and pale green parts only; to be sliced into circles)
- ¼ cup dry white wine (or chicken bone broth)
- ¾ lb. cremini mushrooms (or button mushrooms; to be sliced ¼ inch thick)
- 1tbsps. arrowroot flour
- ¼ cup almond milk (plain and unsweetened)
- scallions (or fresh parsley, to garnish; optional)

Instructions

1. Pat the chicken dry using the paper towel and season with pepper and salt.
2. Start the Instant Pot on the "Sauté" mode and add butter or ghee when hot. When the butter or ghee melts, add the chicken to brown on both sides. After about 3-5 minutes, transfer the chicken breasts to a plate.
3. Add wine or broth and deglaze by scraping up any brown bits using a wooden spoon and stirring. Keep sautéing for 1 or 2 minutes.
4. Add the leeks and mushrooms and with the chicken breasts and juices.

5. Select the "Pressure Cook" / "Manual" setting and set to cook on High Pressure for 8 minutes.
6. When the pot beeps, do a natural pressure release for 4 minutes and then quick-release the remaining pressure.
7. Remove the chicken from the pot to a plate and stir in arrowroot to the almond milk and sauté all in the Instant Pot on high heat. Stir occasionally as it cooks for about 2 minutes for to thicken
8. Serve the breasts on leeks and mushrooms.

Chicken Lazone

- **Prep Time:**   10 minutes
- **Cook Time:**   3 minutes
- **Yields:**   2-3 servings

Ingredients

- 1 tsp. garlic powder
- ½ tsp. onion powder
- ½ tsp. chili powder
- ½ tsp. paprika
- ½ tsp. salt (or to taste)
- ½ tsp. pepper (or to taste)
- 1 lb. chicken tenders
- 1 tbsp. butter
- 1 tbsp. oil
- ¼ cup chicken broth
- 1 tbsp. cornstarch
- 1 tbsp. water
- 1 cup heavy cream
- 1 tbsp. parsley (fresh, finely chopped)
- 5-6 oz. spaghetti

Instructions

1. Combine and mix well the first 6 ingredients on the list including and up to pepper in a mixing bowl. Toss in the chicken with your hands with the spices.
2. Press the "Sauté" button on the Instant Pot to preheat it. Add the butter and oil to the hot pot and melt. Sauté the chicken on both sides to brown and transfer to a plate.
3. Add the broth to the pot and deglaze if you need to.
4. Secure the lid in place and set the pot to "Manual" / "Pressure Cook" and to cook and high pressure for 3 minutes. Once the timer beeps, quick-release the pressure.

5. Stir in the cornstarch to the water in a small bowl and add to the pot with the chicken pushed to one side of the pot. Then stir well the mixture to combine well.
6. Start sautéing one more time until the sauce thickens. Then press "Cancel" to stop sautéing and stir in the heavy cream.
7. Serve the chicken and sauce on the spaghetti prepared according to the package instructions.

CHAPTER 6: THE INSTANT POT FISH AND SEAFOOD RECIPES FOR BEGINNERS

Shrimps, lobsters, salmons, mussels, and cods all have one thing in common. They, like fish, are nice seafood that have been parts of cuisines the world over. You surely like to try your culinary skills on some of them. The Instant Pot can help you to make them as tasty as they can ever be. That's why efforts have been made to include some of them in these Instant Pot recipes for two. You may make some adjustment to the recipes and instructions here as seafood are generally versatile.

Shrimp Scampi

- **Prep Time:**   5 minutes
- **Cook Time:**   8 minutes
- **Yields:**   2 servings

Ingredients

- ¼ cup dry white wine (of any kind) or dry vermouth
- 1 tbsp. butter
- 1 tbsp. olive oil
- 2 tsp. peeled and minced garlic
- ¼ tsp. dried oregano
- ¼ tsp. red pepper flakes
- 1 lb. frozen raw medium shrimp (peeled and deveined; about 30-35)

Instructions

1. Mix all the ingredients apart from shrimp in the Instant Pot. Stir well to combine and then add the shrimp. Stir well.
2. The first option is to cook using the Max Pressure Cooker; press "Pressure Cook" on Max pressure for 5 minutes. The "Keep Warm" setting should be off.
3. If cooking on All Pressure Cooker, select "Pressure Cook" / "Manual" and cook on High Pressure for 8 minutes. The "Keep Warm" setting should be off with the vent closed.
4. When the cooking is done, do the quick release of pressure.
5. Unlatch to open the lid. Transfer the shrimp and sauce into a bowl. Then serve hot.

Sweet and Sour Shrimp

- **Prep Time:**   5 minutes
- **Cook Time:**   15 minutes
- **Yields:**   2-3 servings

Ingredients

- ½ cup canned drained chunks of pineapple in juice (plus another ¼ cup juice from the can)
- ¼ cup chicken broth (or vegetable broth or fish broth)
- ¼ cup regular soy sauce (or reduced-sodium, or tamari)
- ¼ cup sugar (granulated, white)
- 1/8 cup rice vinegar (unseasoned or 1 ½ tbsps. apple cider vinegar)
- ½ tbsp. peeled and minced fresh ginger
- 1 tsp. peeled and minced garlic
- ¼ tsp. red pepper flakes (or to taste)
- 1 lb. frozen raw medium shrimp (peeled and deveined, 30–35)
- ½ lb. frozen stir-fry vegetable blend (unseasoned, 2 to 3 cups, discard any seasoning packet)
- 1 tbsp. cornstarch

Instructions

1. In the Instant Pot, combine the drained pineapple chunks (not the juice), the broth, soy sauce, granulated sugar, vinegar, garlic, ginger, and pepper flakes and stir well to mix. Then add the shrimp and vegetable. Stir well to combine in the pot.
2. Lock the lid into place and cook on Max pressure for 12 minutes. The "Keep Warm" setting should be off. That is if you're cooking on the Max Pressure Cooker. If you're cooking on All Pressure Cooker, select "Pressure Cook" / "Manual" and cook on High Pressure for 13 minutes. The "Keep Warm" setting should be off while the vent is closed.
3. Once the time is up, turn the vent valve to the "Venting" position for a quick release of pressure. When pressure is back to normal, open the pot and select "Sauté" function on "Medium", "Normal", or "Custom 300° F" with the time set for 5 minutes.
4. Bring the sauce to a simmer. Meanwhile, whisk the pineapple juice and the cornstarch in a bowl until smooth. Add the mixture into the sauce and stir as it simmers. Continue to stir constantly for 1 minute or until thickened.
5. Turn off the "Sauté" mode. Use a kitchen mitt to remove the insert from the pot as the shrimp can overcook.
6. Then pour the sauce and shrimp into a serving bowl and serve.

Thai Shrimp Curry

- **Prep Time:**   15 minutes
- **Cook Time:**   25 minutes
- **Yields:**   2 servings

Ingredients

- ½ can coconut milk (7 oz., freeze the rest for another day)
- 1 ½ Thai chili (to be stemmed, seeded, and chopped)
- ¼ cup cilantro leaves (fresh)
- 3 garlic cloves (to be peeled and smashed)
- 1 lemongrass stalk (to be trimmed to bottom, 6 inches and chopped)
- 1 1-inch piece ginger (to be peeled and chopped)
- ½ tbsp. fish sauce
- 1 tsp. packed brown sugar
- 1 tsp. grated lime zest (plus lime wedges, for serving)
- 1 tsp. ground cumin
- 3 oz. sugar snap peas (strings removed)
- 1 red bell pepper (stemmed, seeded, cut into ½-inch pieces)
- 1 tsp. vegetable oil
- ½ lb. large shrimp (peeled, deveined, tails removed)
- ¼ cup fresh Thai basil leaves
- Lime wedges

Instructions

1. Combine the first 10 ingredients on the list in an Ace blender and lock the lid in place. Blend on "High Speed" until smooth, which is about 2 minutes. Scrape down all sides of the jar for a complete yield. Return the lid and for chunky soups, select "Soup Program 1".
2. In the meantime, add snap peas, red bell pepper, and vegetable oil in a microwave-safe oven and microwave for 3 minutes or until the vegetable starts softening. Then drain and set aside.
3. Pause the "Soup Program" 12 minutes to the end and carefully remove the lid. Stir in the microwaved snap peas, red bell peppers, and shrimp into the sauce. Let them be fully submerged.
4. Then return the lid and use food tamper to replace the lid cap.
5. Now resume the "Soup Program" and stir the ingredients when needed, with the tamper.
6. Once the program ends, stir in the basil, and season with salt to taste, and then serve with lime wedges.

Champagne Lobster Risotto

- **Prep Time:**   0 minutes
- **Cook Time:**   35 minutes
- **Yields:**   2 servings

Ingredients

- ¼ cup water
- ¼ cup champagne
- 4 oz. lobster tail meat
- 1 tbsp. butter (+ 1 tsp.)
- ½ tbsp. extra-virgin olive oil
- ½ large shallot (to be peeled and minced)
- ½ leek (to be sliced and rinsed well)
- 1 clove garlic (to be minced)
- ½ cup Arborio rice
- 1/3 cup champagne
- 1 cup fish (or seafood) stock
- 1 ½ tbsps. Mascarpone cheese
- ½ tsp. kosher salt (or to taste)
- ¼ tsp. white pepper
- ½ tsp. lemon juice
- Fresh thyme leaves (as desired, for garnish)

Instructions

1. With the steam rack inside an Instant Pot, pour in ¼ cup of water and ¼ cup of champagne. Arrange the lobster tails on the steam rack and close the lid by latching and ensuring that the vent is closed.
2. Select the "Pressure Cook" / "Manual" on the display panel and program the Instant Pot to 4 minutes of cooking using the "+/-" keys. When the pot beeps, do the quick release of pressure. Transfer the lobster tails to a shallow dish and cover with foil. Take the rack out and discard the juice.
3. Restart the Instant Pot on the "Sauté" function from the display panel and add 1 tablespoon of butter and olive oil when hot to melt. Then add shallots and leeks. Sauté for 2-3 minutes until soft. Then add garlic and continue sautéing for about 3 minutes more. Add rice and cook for yet another 2-3 minutes.
4. Add 1/3 cup of champagne and stock to the pot. Use a wooden spoon to scrape any brown bits from the pot's bottom to deglaze. Select "Cancel" to turn off the pot. Secure the lid with the vent closed. Then select "Pressure Cook" / "Manual" on the display panel and set the cook time to 10 minutes using the "+/-" keys.

5. In the meantime, melt the remaining 1 tablespoon of butter in a small bowl. Crack the lobster shell and pry out the meat. Roughly chop and toss with the melted butter and lemon juice.
6. When the time is up, do the quick pressure release. Open and add mascarpone cheese, white pepper, and salt. Stir to the desired consistency.
7. Serve the risotto with lobster as a topping and fresh thyme as a sprinkle.

Southern Shrimp and Grits

- **Prep Time:**   5 minutes
- **Cook Time:**   40 minutes
- **Yields:**   2 servings

Ingredients **(for grits mixture)**

- ¼ cup grits (not instant)
- 1 cup milk
- 1 tsp. kosher salt (or to taste)
- ¼ tsp. pepper (or to taste)

Ingredients **(for shrimp mixture)**

- 1 lb. shrimp (peeled, deveined, patted dry)
- 1 tsp. Old Bay seasoning
- 1 ½ strip smoked bacon (diced)
- ¼ cup red bell peppers (diced)
- ¼ onion (finely diced)
- ½ tbsp. garlic (minced)
- ¼ cup chicken broth
- 1 tbsp. white wine
- Lemon juice
- 7 oz. diced tomatoes (not drained)
- ¼ tsp. kosher salt (or to taste)
- ¼ tsp. pepper

Ingredients **(to finish)**

- ½ tbsp. butter
- ¼ cup heavy cream
- ½ tbsp. hot sauce (or to taste)
- 1-2 scallions (for topping, sliced, green parts only)

Instructions

1. Whisk together all grits mixture ingredients in a casserole and set aside. Season the shrimp with Old Bay and also set aside.
2. Add the bacon to the pot and set it to "Sauté" mode. Stir as it cooks until crisp. Use a slotted spoon to transfer the bacon to a plate lined with a paper towel.
3. Add red bell peppers and diced onion and continue to cook until soft, about 2 minutes. Then add garlic and cook for 1 minute more.
4. Add broth, white wine, and lemon juice at once. Deglaze by scraping the brown bits from the pot's bottom, using a wooden spoon. Stir in the tomatoes, pepper, and salt.
5. Then insert the steam rack or riser into the pot and gently lower the casserole onto the rack. Tightly secure the lid and ensure that the vent is closed. From the display panel, select the "Pressure Cook" / "Manual" function and program it to cook for 10 minutes, using the "+/-" keys.
6. When the cook time is up, allow 7 minutes of natural pressure releases and then do a quick release of the remaining pressure.
7. Remove the lid when the pressure is fully released and take the casserole and the steam rack out of the pot. Set aside.
8. Add the shrimp to the pot and stir well. Then close the lid tightly to allow the residual heat to cook the shrimp.
9. In the meantime, add ½ tablespoon of butter to the grits. Fluff with a fork until the desired consistency.
10. Stir the heavy cream into the pot to coat the shrimps until they are no longer opaque. Return the cooker to the "Sauté" mode so all can heat through.
11. Finally, add hot sauce to the taste and serve with shrimp over the grit. Top with crumbled bacon and green onions.

CheMeen Kari - Kerala Shrimp Curry

- **Prep Time:**   10 minutes
- **Cook Time:**   10 minutes
- **Yields:**   2-3 servings

Ingredients

- 1-2 tbsp. coconut oil
- ½ tsp. mustard seeds
- 5-6 curry leaves
- ½ medium red onion (to be chopped)
- ½ tbsp. grated fresh ginger
- 1 tsp. ground coriander
- 1-2 cardamom pods
- ½ cinnamon stick
- ½ tsp. cayenne pepper powder

- 2 small tomatoes (to be chopped)
- 1 lb. shrimp (shelled and deveined)
- ¼ cup coconut milk
- ½ tbsp. chopped cilantro

Instructions

1. Set the Instant Pot on the "Sauté" function. And add coconut oil when hot. Add the mustard to the heated oil and stir.
2. When the mustard seeds start to crackle, add the curry leaves, onion, and ginger. Sauté lightly for about 3 minutes.
3. Stir in the next five ingredients, from the coriander to tomatoes. Cook until the tomatoes soften. Then stir in the deveined shrimp and coconut milk. Select "Cancel" to turn off the "Sauté" mode.
4. Close the lid securely with the release valve on the "Sealing" position. Set the pot to "Manual" / "Low Pressure" and cook for 2 minutes.
5. Do a quick release of pressure once the timer beeps.
6. Open the lid and stir well, adding the curry and garnish with the cilantro when serving.

Lightened-Up Shrimp and Grits

- **Prep Time:**   10 minutes
- **Cook Time:**   27 minutes
- **Yields:**   2 servings

Ingredients

- ½ tbsp. olive oil
- 1 tbsp. unsalted butter (divided)
- 6 oz. large shrimp (raw, peeled, deveined)
- ½ clove garlic
- ¼ cup fire-roasted red peppers (to be chopped)
- ¼ tsp. smoked paprika
- ¼ tsp. kosher salt (or to taste)
- 1tsp. fresh thyme (chopped)
- ¼ tsp. red pepper flakes
- ¼ lemon (juiced)
- ¼ cup coarse grits
- 1 cup water
- ¼ cup sharp Cheddar cheese (grated)

- 1 tbsp. sliced scallions

Instructions

1. Start the Instant Pot on the "Sauté" function and add the olive oil and half of the butter to the pot.
2. Add shrimp to the pot, followed by garlic, and leave for 2 minutes to sauté. Then add the red pepper and season with smoked paprika, salt, thyme, red pepper flakes, and lemon. Continue sautéing for 3-5 minutes more or until the shrimp becomes opaque. Select "Cancel" to stop sautéing.
3. Remove the shrimp from the pot and place in a medium bowl to be covered with aluminum foil. Set aside.
4. Combine the grits and the other half of butter in the pot and stir in the water.
5. Securely lock the lid and ensure that the steam release handle is flipped to the "Sealing" position. Press the "Pressure Cook" / "Manual" button and cook on High pressure for 10 minutes.
6. When the timer beeps, wait for 10 minutes for the pressure to be naturally released.
7. Unlatch the lid and open the cooker to add the cheese. Stir constantly until the cheese melts and the grits turn creamy.
8. Serve hot in a serving bowl and top with shrimp and sauce with scallions as the garnish.

Mediterranean Fish Stew

- **Prep Time:**   8 minutes
- **Cook Time:**   18 minutes
- **Yields:**   2 servings

Ingredients

- 4 tsps. olive oil
- 2 cloves garlic (to be minced)
- 1 cup chopped onion
- 1 red bell pepper (to be cut into 2-inch pieces)
- 1 green bell pepper (to be cut into 2-inch pieces)
- 1 potato (to be halved)
- 1 tsp. smoked paprika
- 2 cups chicken broth
- 8 oz. cod fillet (thawed, if frozen)
- 14 ½ oz. diced tomatoes
- ½ cup small cooked shrimp (thawed)
- 2 lemon wedge

- 2 tbsps. fresh dill (chopped)
- ½ cup fresh parsley (chopped)

Instructions

1. Start the Instant Pot on the "Sauté" mode and put on "Normal". Add oil to the hot pot and melt.
2. Add the garlic and onion to the heated oil and stir frequently as they cook for 3 minutes or begin to soften. Add the green and red bell peppers, potato, paprika, broth, and tomatoes.
3. Then close the lid securely with the vent also closed. Press the "Stew" button and set the temperature to "Normal" and the timer to 5 minutes.
4. Once the pot beeps, quick release the pressure. And when the pressure is back to normal, open the cooker and add the fillet. Close the lid back and ensure that the vent is closed. Press the "Stew" button again but this time set to cook on "Less" for 8 minutes.
5. Again, do the quick release of pressure when the time is up. When the pressure is down, open the lid to add the shrimp. Stir well and close tightly for 5 minutes without turning it on. The residual heat will heat the shrimp through.
6. Then serve in a large bowl with herbs and lemon wedge as garnishes.

Lemon Dill Salmon

- **Prep Time:**   3 minutes
- **Cook Time:**   5 minutes
- **Yields:**   2 servings

Ingredients

- 2 salmon fillets (1-inch thick, 3 oz.)
- 1 tsp. fresh dill (chopped)
- ½ tsp. salt (or to taste)
- ¼ tsp. pepper (or to taste)
- 1 cup water
- 2 tbsps. lemon juice
- ½ lemon (to be sliced)

Instructions

1. Sprinkle the salmon filets with dill, pepper, and salt.
2. Position the steam rack in the Instant Pot and add water to the pot.
3. Set the salmon on the rack with the skin side down. Then squeeze the lemon over the filets to extract the juice. Drop the lemon slices on the filet.

4. Tightly close the lid and flip the steam release valve to the "Sealing" position. Then, select the "Steam" function and set the time to 5 minutes.
5. When the timer beeps, do the quick release of the pressure. Then check with the meat thermometer whether the fish is up to 145° F hot. That's when it is completely cooked.
6. Serve with the remaining dill and lemon slices.

Seafood Stew

- **Prep Time:**   10 minutes
- **Cook Time:**   10 minutes
- **Yields:**   2-3 servings

Ingredients

- 1 ½ tbsps. extra-virgin olive oil
- 1 bay leaf
- 1 tsp. paprika
- ½ small onion (to be thinly sliced)
- ½ small green bell pepper (to be thinly sliced)
- 1 cup tomatoes (diced)
- 1 clove garlic (to be smashed)
- Sea salt (to taste)
- Pepper (freshly ground, to taste)
- ½ cup fish stock
- 1 lb. meaty fish (like cod or striped bass, to be cut into 2-inch chunks)
- ½ lb. shrimp (to be cleaned and deveined)
- 6 littleneck clams
- ¼ cup cilantro (for garnish)
- ½ tbsp. extra-virgin olive oil (to add when serving)

Instructions

1. Start the Instant Pot by pressing the "Sauté" function. When the message "hot" appears on the display panel, add olive oil.
2. Add the bay leaf and paprika. Stir for about 20 seconds. Then add onion, sliced bell pepper, tomatoes, garlic, and 1 tablespoon of cilantro. Season with pepper and salt and stir for 2 – 3 minutes occasionally. Add the stock or water.
3. Nestle the neck clams and shrimps among the veggies in the IP. Top everything with the fish pieces.
4. Tightly close the lid and ensure that the steam release is on the "Sealing" position. Select "Pressure Cook" or "Manual" and use the "+/-" button to set the time to 10 minutes.

5. After the timer beeps, wait for 10 minutes for the pressure to release naturally. Then manually release the remaining pressure, if any, by flipping the steam release valve to "Venting".

6. Transfer the stew into bowls and drizzle with the rest of the olive oil, sprinkle with the remaining cilantro, and serve immediately.

Mussels Frites

- **Prep Time:**   30 minutes
- **Cook Time:**   20 minutes
- **Yields:**   2-3 servings

Ingredients **(For Frites)**
- ½ tbsp. rosemary (chopped, fresh)
- ¾ tsp. garlic powder
- ½ tsp. salt (or to taste)
- ¼ tsp. black pepper
- 1 lb. russet potatoes (or gold potatoes, to be cut into ½-inch thick sticks)
- 1 ½ tbsps. olive oil

Ingredients **(For Mussels)**
- ½ cup white wine
- 1 ½ Roma tomatoes (to be seeded and chopped)
- 1 clove garlic (to be minced)
- 1 bay leaf
- 1 lb. mussels (scrubbed and debearded)
- ¼ cup flat-leaf parsley (chopped fresh)

Ingredients **(Dipping Sauce)**
- ¼ cup mayonnaise
- 1 tbsp. red pepper (roasted, minced)
- ½ clove garlic (to be minced)

Instructions

1. Preheat the oven to 450°F. Meanwhile, add rosemary, garlic powder, pepper, and salt in a small bowl. Also, toss the potatoes with oil and spice mixture on a large baking sheet or medium roasting pan. Allow it to roast in the oven for 25 to 30 minutes or until browned and tender. Stir it once.

2. Add the wine, garlic, Roma tomatoes, and bay leaf in the Instant Pot and top with the mussels. Secure the lid and unlatch on the pot. Ensure that the steam release valve is on the "Sealing" position.

3. Press "Pressure Cook" / "Manual" and cook for 3 minutes at High. Depressurize by using a quick-release method.
4. To prepare the dipping sauce, combine the mayonnaise, red pepper, and garlic in a small bowl.
5. Everything is ready; enjoy your mussel's Frites.

Thai Seafood Curry

- **Prep Time:**   10 minutes
- **Cook Time:**   16 minutes
- **Yields:**   2-3 servings

Ingredients

- 1 tbsp. oil. (peanut, coconut oil, or any of avocado, canola, corn, grape, safflower, or vegetable seed)
- 1 cup. chopped allium aromatics
- ¼ cup peeled fresh ginger (minced)
- 1 tbsp. wet curry paste
- 7 oz. diced tomatoes
- ½ cup regular (or low-fat) coconut milk
- 1 tbsp. fresh lime juice
- 1 tbsp. light brown sugar
- 1 tbsp. fish sauce
- 1 lb. fish or shellfish
- ½ lb. chopped quick-cooking vegetables

Instructions

1. Start the Instant Pot on the "Sauté" mode with the time set for 10 minutes.
2. Add the oil to warm for about 2 minutes and add allium aromatics. Stir often for about 2-4 minutes to soften. Add the ginger, cook for a few seconds until aromatic.
3. Add the curry paste until everything is coated. Add tomatoes, coconut milk, fresh lime, sugar, and sauce. Stir everything for a few minutes until the brown sugar dissolves. Press "Cancel" to turn off the sauté mode. Lock the lid securely onto the pot.
4. If you're cooking on the Max Pressure Cooker, select "Pressure Cook" on Max for 5 minutes, ensure that the "Keep Warm" setting is off.
5. If you're cooking on All Pressure Cookers, select "Meat" / "Stew" / "Pressure Cook"/ "Manual" and set to 7 minutes, ensure that the "Keep Warm" setting is off.

6. Once the cook time elapses, either way, do the quick release of pressure to bring the pressure back to normal.
7. Unlatch the lid and open the pot. Then switch to the "Sauté" mode for the next 5 minutes to bring the sauce to simmer. Add the fish or shellfish and stir. Add quick-cooking vegetables.
8. Continue sautéing for about 3-5 minutes until the fish or shellfish is fully cooked, stir gently.
9. Press "Cancel" to stop sautéing.
10. Use tongs to remove the hot insert from the pot and serve hot.

Asiago Shrimp Risotto

- **Prep Time:**   5 minutes
- **Cook Time:**   25 minutes
- **Yields:**   2 servings

Ingredients

- 1 ½ tbsp. butter
- ½ small yellow onion (to be finely chopped) clove garlic (to be minced)
- 1 cup Arborio rice
- 1 tbsp. dry white wine
- 2 cups chicken broth (1 ½ cups + ½ cup divided)
- ½ tsp. kosher salt (or to taste)
- ¼ tsp. pepper (or to taste)
- ½ lb. medium shrimp (thawed, peeled, deveined)
- ¼ cup asiago cheese (grated)
- 1/4 cup flat-leaf parsley (finely chopped)
- 1 tbsp. fresh tarragon (or 1 tsp. dried tarragon)

Instructions

1. Start the Instant Pot on the "Sauté" function and add butter to the hot pot.
2. Add onion and garlic when the butter melts. Cook and stir well for 3 minutes or until onion is softened. Add rice and cook for 1 minute more, stir well.
3. Quickly deglaze by adding wine to the pot and scraping the brown bits from the bottom with a wooden spoon. Add 2 cups of chicken broth, pepper, and salt. Stir well to combine.
4. Put on the lid and secure by latching and flipping the steam release valve to the "Sealing" position.

5. Select the "Pressure Cook" / "Manual" on the display panel and program the pot to cook for 12 minutes using the "+/-" keys.
6. When the cook time is up, do the quick release of the pressure. Select "Cancel" to turn off the pot and start again on the "Sauté" mode.
7. Add the shrimp, stir, and add the remaining ½ cup of broth. Keep stirring occasionally for 3 – 5 minutes until the shrimp turn opaque. Add the cheese and stir in until melted.
8. Fold in herbs and serve immediately.

Garlic Butter Shrimp With Broccoli

- **Prep Time:**   5 minutes
- **Cook Time:**   10 minutes
- **Yields:**   2 servings

Ingredients

- 1 tbsp. butter
- 1 shallot (finely diced)
- ½ tbsp. garlic (to be minced)
- ¼ cup white wine
- ¼ cup chicken broth
- 1 tbsp. lemon juice
- ¼ tsp. kosher salt (or to taste)
- ¼ tsp. pepper
- 1 lb. shrimp (not frozen, deveined and peeled)
- 1 ¼ cups bite-size broccoli florets
- 1 tbsp. grated parmesan cheese (additional for garnish)

Instructions

1. Start the Instant Pot on the "Sauté" function and add butter to the hot pot.
2. Add the shallot when the butter melts. Cook and stir well for 3 minutes. Add the garlic and cook for 1 minute more, stir well.
3. Quickly deglaze by adding wine to the pot and scraping the brown bits from the bottom with a wooden spoon.
4. Add broth, lemon, pepper, and salt and stir to combine. Then, stir in the shrimp.
5. Layer the broccoli evenly on the pot without stirring.
6. Select "Cancel" to turn off the pot. Put on the lid and secure by latching and flipping the steam release valve to the "Sealing" position.
7. Select the "Pressure Cook" / "Manual" on the display panel and program the pot to cook for 10 minutes using the "+/-" keys.

8. When the cook time is up, do the quick release of the pressure.
9. Add the parmesan cheese, stir well and serve immediately garnished with additional cheese, if you like.

CHAPTER 7: THE INSTANT POT VEGAN/VEGETARIAN RECIPES FOR BEGINNERS

Even vegans can have their nice meals cooked in the Instant Pot despite their aversion for fish and meats. There are a lot of wonders that can come from grains, seeds, and vegetables if you take them through this pressure cooker. Even though the size of the meal may not have a significant effect on the cooking time, it does on the prepping. Here are some recipes for two for some of these vegetarian meals.

Chai Spiced Rice Pudding

- **Prep Time:**   5 minutes
- **Cook Time:**   30 minutes
- **Yields:**   2 servings

Ingredients

- ½ cup medium-grain rice
- 1 cup unsweetened plain almond milk (or other nondairy milk, like soy or oat milk)
- ½ cup canned coconut milk (full-fat, well stirred)
- ½ cup water
- ½ tsp. pure vanilla extract
- 1/8 tsp. kosher salt (or to taste)
- 1 tsp. ground cinnamon
- ½ tsp. ground ginger
- ¼ tsp. ground cardamom
- ¼ tsp. freshly grated (or ground nutmeg)
- 1/8 tsp. ground cloves
- 1tbsp almond butter (no-added-sugar)
- ½ tbsp. pure maple syrup (or coconut sugar)
- 2 soft Medjool dates (pitted, roughly torn into pieces)

Ingredients (for roasted grapes, optional)

- ½ bunch of seedless grapes
- Olive oil
- Kosher salt (or sea salt)
- Leaves (fresh thyme)

Instructions

1. Preheat the oven to 450ºF and add the roasted grapes (if using).
2. Meanwhile, to make the rice pudding; pour the rice into the Instant Pot and add almond milk, well-stirred coconut milk, vanilla, water, cinnamon, cardamom, ginger, nutmeg, maple syrup, almond butter, cloves, dates, and salt. Stir well for all to combine.

3. Tightly secure the lid with the steam release valve turned to the "Sealing" position. Press the "Pressure Cook" / "Manual" function and set to cook at high pressure for 10 minutes.
4. While the oven is heating up, prepare the roasted grape by arranging the grapes on a rimmed baking sheet. Drizzle with olive oil. Sprinkle with salt and thyme leaves. Gently toss with hands. Then bake in the oven for 8 to 9 minutes or when the grapes are beginning to burst.
5. By now, the Instant Pot timer must have beeped after 10 minutes, wait for another 10 minutes of natural pressure release and switch the release valve to the "Venting" position for the quick release of the remaining pressure.
6. Unlatch the lid to open and stir the rice pudding well to incorporate any extra liquid. Transfer the pudding to bowls and serve with the roasted grapes, if using.

Israeli Couscous and Lentils

- **Prep Time:**   10 minutes
- **Cook Time:**   15 minutes
- **Yields:**   2 servings

Ingredients (for Couscous and Lentils)
- ½ cup French green lentils (Puy)
- ½ medium yellow onion (to be diced)
- 1 red yellow bell peppers (or orange, to be diced)
- 1 carrot (diced)
- 3 garlic cloves (to be minced)
- ½ cup Israeli couscous (or pearl)
- 1 ¾ cups vegetable broth (low sodium)
- 1 tsp. kosher salt (to taste)
- Black pepper (freshly cracked)
- 1 bay leaf
- A handful of fresh thyme sprigs

Ingredients (to Finish)
- 1 ¼ tbsp. extra-virgin olive oil
- 1 tbsp. red wine vinegar
- ½ cup fresh dill (finely chopped)
- ½ cup fresh Italian parsley (flat-leaf, finely chopped)
- 7-8 pitted green olives (to be sliced)
- 1-pint cherry tomatoes (to be halved or quartered)
- Freshly cracked black pepper (to taste)
- Kosher salt (to taste)

Instructions

1. Submerge the lentils completely in water overnight or at least 8 hours.
2. Drain and place the soaked lentils and the remaining ingredients for couscous and lentils in the Instant Pot. Stir well to combine.
3. Latch the lid to secure and set the steam release knob to the "Sealing" position. Select the "Pressure Cook" / "Manual" setting and cook at High Pressure for 3 minutes.
4. When the timer beeps, allow 10 minutes of natural pressure release and then switch the release knob to the "Venting" position for a quick release of any remaining pressure.
5. Open the lid and discard the bay leaf and thyme sprigs inside the pot.
6. Pour the mixture into a serving bowl and allow it to cool down to room temperature.
7. Then combine all ingredients for finishing and stir well while tasting for appropriateness of seasoning. Add this to the couscous and lentil mixture. You can add more pepper and salt if needed, and a splash of vinegar for acidity.

Creamy Veggie Risotto

- **Prep Time:**   4 minutes
- **Cook Time:**   12 minutes
- **Yields:**   2-3 servings

Ingredients
- 1 tbsp. olive oil
- ¼ sweet onion (to be diced)
- ½ garlic clove (to be minced)
- ½ bunch asparagus tips (to be cut into 1-inch pieces)
- 1 ½ cups DIY Vegetable Stock (or store-bought stock)
- ½ cup Arborio rice (to be rinsed and drained)
- ½ cup sugar snap peas (to be rinsed, tough ends removed)
- ½ tsp. dried thyme
- ½ tsp. salt (or to taste)
- ¼ tsp. freshly ground black pepper (or to taste)
- Pinch red pepper flakes
- 1 tbsp. vegan butter
- ½ lemon (to be juiced)
- 1 ½ cups fresh baby spinach (torn)

Instructions

1. Start your Instant Pot on the "Sauté" / "Low" mode. When the message "Hot" displays on the panel, add the oil and heat to shimmering.
2. Add the onion and stir frequently as it cooks for 2 - 3 minutes. Turn off the Instant Pot by pressing "Cancel".
3. Add the garlic and asparagus and stir as it cooks for 30 seconds.

4. Add the next 7 ingredients as listed from the stock to red pepper flakes. Stir well to combine.
5. Lock the lid in place and switch the steam release knob to the "Sealing" position. Select the "Pressure Cook" / "Manual" option and set to cook on High Pressure with the time set for 8 minutes.
6. Once the timer beeps, shift the knob to the "Venting" position for a quick release of the pressure.
7. Unlatch to remove the lid. Gently stir in the last 3 ingredients; avoid tearing the snap peas. Adjust the seasoning as desired and serve.

Fruity Quinoa & Granola Bowls

- **Prep Time:**   2 minutes
- **Cook Time:**   8 minutes
- **Yields:**   2 servings

Ingredients

- ½ cup quinoa (to be rinsed)
- ¾ cup water
- 1 tbsp. maple syrup (plus more for topping, optional)
- 1 tsp. vanilla extract
- ¼ tsp. ground cinnamon
- Pinch salt (to taste)
- ¼ - ½ cup nondairy milk
- 1 cup granola (any variety)
- 1 cup Fresh Fruit Compote
- Sliced bananas (for topping, optional)
- Toasted walnuts (for topping, optional)

Instructions

1. Combine the first 6 ingredients on the recipe list in the Instant Pot and mix well.
2. Tightly secure the lid and turn the steam release knob to the "Sealing" position. Select the "Pressure Cook" / "Manual" function, set to cook on High Pressure for 8 minutes.
3. When the cook time elapses, wait 10 minutes for the pressure to release naturally. Then do a quick release any remaining pressure.
4. Carefully remove the lid, stir the quinoa mixture and add enough milk to the desired consistency.
5. Spoon the quinoa mixture into bowls and serve topped with granola, compote, and other desired additional toppings.

Massaman Curry With Tofu and Kabocha Squash

- **Prep Time:**   2 minutes
- **Cook Time:**   9 minutes
- **Yields:**   2 servings

Ingredients

- 7 oz. tofu 1 block firm (to be drained)
- ½ tbsp. coconut oil
- 1 small yellow onion (to be cut into 1-inch pieces)
- ¼ cup coconut cream
- 1/8 cup Massaman curry paste
- ½ cup vegetable broth (low sodium)
- ½ Kabocha squash (to be seeded, cut into 1-inch cubes)
- ½ cup coconut milk
- ½ cup fresh Thai basil leaves (loosely packed)
- Hot steamed rice (for serving)

Instructions

1. Slice the tofu into ½-inch pieces. Cover each slice with double layers of paper towels (you can use a folded kitchen towel) and exert a firm pressure to de-moisturize as much as possible. Cut each slice into ½-inch cubes and set aside.
2. Start the Instant Pot on the "High Sauté" and add the coconut oil. Add the onion when the oil has melted and sauté for about 4 minutes or until the onion begins to brown. Pour in the coconut cream and addthe curry paste. Sauté for about 2 minutes to let it bubble and fragrant. Deglaze by stir in the broth and using a wooden spoon to nudge screap any brown bits from the bottom of the pot. Then add the squash in one single layer.
3. Tightly secure the lid with the steam release valve set to the "Sealing" position. Press the "Cancel" button to stop sautéing and reset the cooking program. Select the "Pressure Cook" / "Manual" setting and with the cook time set to 1 minute, cook at Low Pressure. (It may take up to 10 minutes before the pot comes to pressure and begins the cooking program.)
4. Once the pot beeps at the end of cooking, do a quick pressure release of pressure by shifting the steam release valve to the "Venting" position. Unlatch the lid to opethe n pot and stir in the coconut milk and add the tofu.
5. Start the cooking program again on the "Sauté" setting. Allow the curry to come up to a simmer, and then cook for 2 minutes. Stirring gently occasionally to avoid breaking up the tofu. Turn off the pot by pressing the "Cancel" button. Then stir in the basil.
6. Pour into bowls and serve hot with the rice.

Red Thai Curry Cauliflower

- **Prep Time:**   10 minutes
- **Cook Time:**   2 minutes
- **Yields:**   2-3 servings

Ingredients

- 7 oz. coconut milk (full fat)
- ¼ - ½ cup water
- 1 tbsp. red curry paste
- ½ tsp. garlic powder
- ½ tsp. salt (or plus more as needed)
- ¼ tsp. ground ginger
- ¼ tsp. onion powder
- ¼ tsp. chili powder (either Thai or cayenne pepper)
- 1 bell pepper (of any color, to be thinly sliced)
- 1 ½ - 2 cups of cauliflower (cut into bite-size pieces)
- 7 oz. can diced tomatoes (and liquid ½ can)
- Freshly ground black pepper
- Cooked rice (or other grain, for serving, optional)

Instructions

1. Stir together the first 8 ingredients on the recipe list in the Instant Pot. Once well combine, add the next 3 and stir again.
2. Tightly secure the lid with the pressure release handle switched to the "Sealing" position. Select "Pressure Cook" / "Manual" setting and with the cook time set to 2 minutes, cook at High Pressure.
3. Once the pot beeps at the end of cooking, do a quick pressure release of pressure by shifting the steam release valve to the "Venting" position.
4. Unlatch the lid to open the pot and stir everything together thoroughly. Taste and, if needed, adjust the seasoning.
5. Then, serve with cooked rice or any other grain (if using).

Smoky Chipotle Quinoa, Black Beans, and Corn

- **Prep Time:**   5 minutes
- **Cook Time:**   5 minutes
- **Yields:**   2-3 servings

Ingredients (Dry)

- ½ tbsp. ground chipotle powder
- 1 tsp. ground cumin
- 1 tbsp. dried onion
- 1 tsp. dried garlic
- 1 tsp. Mexican oregano
- ¼ tsp. sea salt (or to taste)
- 1 cups quick-cooking quinoa
- ½ cup dehydrated black beans
- ¼ cup dried corn

Ingredients (For Cooking and Serving)

- 2 cups vegetable broth (or water)
- Roughly chopped fresh cilantro (to serve)
- Lime juice (to serve)

Instructions

1. Layer all the dry ingredients in a jar in the listed order.
2. Add the broth or water to the jarred ingredients in the Instant Pot and stir well to combine.
3. Tightly secure the lid with the pressure release handle switched to the "Sealed" position. Select "Pressure Cook" / "Manual" setting and with the cook time set to 5 minutes, cook on High Pressure.
4. When the timer beeps, wait for another 5 minutes for the natural pressure release. Then shift the pressure handle to the "Venting" position for a quick and manual release of any remaining pressure.
5. Serve garnished with fresh cilantro with a squeeze of lime juice.

Herb and Lemon Orzo With Peas

- **Prep Time:**   5 minutes
- **Cook Time:**   5 minutes
- **Yields:**   2 servings

Ingredients (Dry)

- 1 ¼ cups dry orzo pasta
- ¼ tsp. sea salt (or to taste)
- ½ tbsp. dried parsley

- ½ tsp. dried thyme
- ½ tsp. dried garlic
- ½ tsp. dried lemon zest
- ½ cup dehydrated peas

Ingredients (For Cooking and Serving)

- 2 cups vegetable broth (or water)
- 1 tbsp. extra-virgin olive oil

Instructions

1. Start preparing by layering all the dry ingredients in a jar in the listed order.
2. Start to cook by adding the broth or water to the jarred ingredients in the Instant Pot and stirring well to combine.
3. Tightly secure the lid with the pressure release handle switched to the "Sealed" position. Select "Pressure Cook" / "Manual" setting, and with the cook time set to 5 minutes, cook on High Pressure.
4. When the timer beeps, wait for another 5 minutes for the natural pressure release. Then shift the pressure handle to the "Venting" position for a quick and manual release of any remaining pressure.
5. Then serve hot and enjoy!

Vegan Southwest Quinoa Bowls

- **Prep Time:**   5 minutes
- **Cook Time:**   15 minutes
- **Yields:**   2-3 servings

Ingredients (Vegan Southwest Quinoa Bowls)

- ½ tsp. extra-virgin olive oil
- ¼ onion (to be diced)
- 1 bell pepper (to be seeded and diced)
- ½ tsp. salt (or to taste)
- ½ tsp. ground cumin
- ½ cup uncooked quinoa (to be rinsed)
- ½ cup salsa (of choice)
- ½ cup water
- 7 ½ oz. black beans (½ can, drained and rinsed)

Ingredients (Toppings)

- Avocado (to be diced)
- Fresh cilantro
- Guacamole
- Green onions
- Lime wedges
- Salsa
- Shredded lettuce

Instructions

1. Start the Instant Pot on the "Sauté" / "Normal" mode and add oil when the message "Hot" is displayed. After heating for about 2 minutes, add the onion and bell pepper. Sauté for 2-3 minutes until they start to soften. Then stir in cumin and salt and cook for 1 minute.
2. Press the "Cancel" button to reset the program. Stir in the quinoa and add salsa and water.
3. Tightly secure the lid with the pressure release handle switched to the "Sealed" position. Select the "Rice" program. When the coingok program ends, allow the natural release of pressure for the quinoa to completely absorb the liquid.
4. Using a fork, fluff the quinoa and stir in the beans.
5. Serve warm, with any or all of the toppings on the recipe listing.

Classic Tomatillo and Árbol Chile Salsa

- **Prep Time:**   5 minutes
- **Cook Time:**   15 minutes
- **Yields:**   2-3 cups

Ingredients

- 1 tbsp. vegetable oil
- 40 dried árbol chiles (stems to be removed)
- 3 cloves garlic (to be peeled)
- 2 ¼ lb. tomatillos (husks to be removed)
- Coarse salt (to taste)
- 2 cups water

Instructions

1. Start the Instant Pot to the "Sauté" mode and adjust to "More" for high.
2. Add the vegetable oil to the pot when the message "Hot" is displayed on the panel.

3. Add the chili and garlic to oil when melted and sauté for about 2 to 3 minutes or until lightly toasted. Then add the tomatillos and water.
4. Tightly secure the lid with the pressure release handle switched to the "Sealed" position. Select "Pressure Cook" / "Manual" setting and with the cook time set to 12 minutes, cook on High Pressure.
5. Once the pot beeps at the end of cooking, do a quick pressure release of pressure by shifting the steam release valve to the "Venting" position.
6. Unlatch the lid to open the cooker.
7. Transfer the tomatillos, chilies, and garlic ta o high power food processor, using a slotted spoon. Pour 1 cup of the cooking liquid into the processor and purée until smooth. Hold the lid down with a mitt or a kitchen towel to avoid a splash of hot sauce.
8. Pour into a bowl to season with salt to taste and serve.

Pea and Paneer Curry

- **Prep Time:**   10 minutes
- **Cook Time:**   20 minutes
- **Yields:**   2 servings

Ingredients

- ¾ cups finely chopped onions
- ½ cup finely chopped tomatoes
- ½ cup water
- 1 tbsp. vegetable oil
- ½ tbsp. fresh ginger (minced)
- ½ tbsp. garlic (minced)
- ½ tsp. ground turmeric
- ½ tsp. garam masala
- ½ tsp. cayenne pepper
- ½ cup paneer soft Indian cheese (chopped)
- ¼ cup heavy cream (or full-fat coconut milk)
- ¼ cup fresh cilantro (or parsley, chopped)
- 6 oz. frozen peas (½ package)

Instructions

1. Combine the first 9 ingredients on the recipe list, up to cayenne pepper, in the Instant Pot and stir well to combine. But reserve ¼ cup of water.
2. Tightly secure the lid with the pressure release handle switched to the "Sealed" position. Select "Pressure Cook" / "Manual" setting, and with the cook time set to 5 minutes, cook on High Pressure.

3. When the timer beeps, wait for another 5 minutes for the natural pressure release. Then shift the pressure handle to the "Venting" position for a quick and manual release of any remaining pressure.
4. Press the "Sauté" button and add the reserved ¼ cup of water to the pot together with paneer, cilantro, cream, and peas. Keep stirring occasionally as you cook for about 5 to 8 minutes, or until heated through.
5. Select "Cancel" to end the "Sauté" program.

Ratatouille With Black Olives and Quinoa

- **Prep Time:**   5 minutes
- **Cook Time:**   10 minutes
- **Yields:**   2 servings

Ingredients

- 5 tsp. olive oil (divided)
- 1 eggplant (quartered lengthwise and chop into then chop into 1-inch pieces)
- ½ medium red onion (to be sliced)
- 2 cloves garlic
- ½ red bell pepper (to be cut into 1-inch pieces)
- ½ green bell pepper (to be cut into 1-inch pieces)
- 2 zucchinis (to be cut into 1-inch pieces)
- 1 tbsp. balsamic vinegar
- 14 ½ oz. diced tomatoes (1 can)
- ½ cup cooked quinoa
- 10 black olives
- ¼ cup torn basil leaves (optional)

Instructions

1. Start the Instant Pot on the "Sauté" program and seit t to Normal. Once the message "Hot" shows on the display panel, add 2 teaspoons of olive oil.
2. Add the eggplant, cook until browned, remove, and then set aside.
3. Add the remaining 3 teaspoons of olive oil together with onion, garlic, bell peppers, and zucchini. Then cook for about 3 minutes while stirring constantly.
4. Add the balsamic vinegar and cook for one minute. Add the diced tomatoes.
5. Tightly close the lid and set the release handle to the "Sealed" position. Select the "Steam" program and set to cook on Normal with the time set to 3 minutes.
6. Once the timer beeps, do the quick release of the pressure and leave again for 2 minutes. Divide the ratatouille into two and remove half to be refrigerated. Serve with basil leaves as a garnish, if desired.

Acorn Squash With Shallots & Grapes

- **Prep Time:**   5 minutes
- **Cook Time:**   25 minutes
- **Yields:**   2 servings

Ingredients

- 1 small acorn squash (cut in half lengthwise, seeds removed)
- 1 tbsp. olive oil
- ½ tbsp. fresh sage (to be chopped)
- ¼ tsp. salt (or to taste)
- ¼ tsp. pepper (or to taste)
- ½ lb. red grapes (approximately 20 grapes)
- 1 medium shallot (peeled and sliced thin crosswise)
- Salt (to taste)
- Ground pepper (to taste)

Instructions

1. Drizzle ½ tablespoon of oil over both halves of the acorn squash. Sprinkle the oiled squash with the chopped sage, pepper, and salt. Set about 10 grapes into the cavities in the squash and sprinkle the grapes with the slices of shallots.
2. Position the steam rack in the inner pot of the Instant Pot and add 1 cup of water. Carefully place both halves of the squash on the steam rack. Set them with the cavity side up.
3. Lock the lid in place and switch the steam release knob to the "Sealing" position. Select "Pressure Cook" / "Manual" and set to 4 minutes.
4. When the time is up, wait for 10 minutes for natural pressure release. Then shift the pressure release handle to the "Venting" position for a quick and manual release of any remaining pressure.
5. Remove the lid when the pressure has returned to the normal position and use the tongs to carefully transfer the squash to bowls.
6. Season with additional pepper and salt to taste and serve immediately.

Eggplant in Cilantro Gravy

- **Prep Time:**   5 minutes
- **Cook Time:**   15 minutes
- **Yields:**   2-3 servings

Ingredients

- 10 eggplants (baby purple)
- ½ tbsp. cumin seeds
- ½ tbsp. mustard seeds
- 1 ½ tbsps. oil (any veggie oil)
- ¼ cup water (or as needed)
- 1 bunch fresh cilantro
- Green chilies (to taste)
- Salt (to taste)
- -1 inch fresh ginger
- 1 inch sized tamarind ball (or 1 ½ tamarind concentrate)

Instructions

1. Grind the cilantro, chilies, and ginger with a minimal amount of water, if using any at all.
2. Wash the eggplants and form crisscross slits up to their ¾th lengths.
3. Stuff the eggplants with the ground cilantro paste along the slits and set aside.
4. Start the Instant Pot on the "Sauté" mode on High. When the message "Hot" is displayed, add oil.
5. Add cumin seeds and mustard seeds to the oil when oil hot. Sauté for 5 minutes or as desired. Turn off the "Sauté" mode.
6. Layer the stuffed eggplants in the pot.
7. Add the rest of the cilantro paste and about ¼ cup of water. Mix gently if you need to.
8. Lock the lid in place and switch the steam release knob to the "Sealing" position. Select "Pressure Cook" / "Manual" and set to cook for10 minutes.
9. When the time is up, shift the pressure handle to the "Venting" position for a quick and manual release of any remaining pressure.

CHAPTER 8: THE INSTANT POT SNACKS AND SIDE DISHES RECIPES FOR BEGINNERS

If you are the type that loves to snack between meals, this chapter is for you. Do you always take delight in decorating your dining moments with good sides besides your main course? You've got to pay attention to this chapter. The list of side dishes that you can make in your Instant Pot is endless. Chefs have experimented with cheeses, veggies, pastas, salads, pizzas, bites, and so on. Some of these have been made into these recipes for two. Check them out in this chapter.

Cheesy Vegetable Strata

- **Prep Time:**   5 minutes
- **Cook Time:**   20 minutes
- **Yields:**   2 servings

Ingredients (Dry)

- ¼ cup dried Parmesan cheese
- 1 tbsp. dried yellow (or green) onion
- ¼ cup green bell pepper (dried)
- 1 tbsp. sundried tomatoes
- ½ tbsp. dried parsley
- ½ tsp. sea salt (or to taste)
- ¼ tsp. ground black pepper
- 2 cups dry cubed bread

Ingredients (for Cooking and Serving)

- Cooking Spray
- 4 eggs
- ¼ cup heavy cream
- ½ cup water

Instructions

1. Start preparation by layering all the dry ingredients in a jar in the listed order.
2. Start cooking by coating the bottom and sides of a medium dish (such as a Pyrex dish) or a fluted tube pan (such as a Bundt pan) with a cooking spray.
3. Set all of the ingredients into a baking dish.
4. Whisk together the eggs and the heavy cream in a separate jar and pour the mixture into the pan. To submerge the bread in the mixture, press down on it. Then stir gently to allow the ingredients to disperse.

5. Using an aluminum pan, cover the pan and pour a cup of water on the Instant Pot with the trivet or steam rack inside. Lower the baking dish into the pot on top of the trivet using a foil sling.
6. Close the lid in place with the vent release knob in the "Sealed" position. Select "Pressure Cook" / "Manual" and cook on High with the time set to 10 minutes.
7. Once the cooker beeps, turn the knob to the "Venting" / "Vent" position to release the pressure manually.
8. Serve as a side to any meal.

Parmesan Puffs 2 Ways

- **Prep Time:**   5 minutes
- **Cook Time:**   10 minutes
- **Yields:**   2 servings

Ingredients (for Parmesan Puffs 2 Ways)

- 1 egg white
- 2 oz. good quality parmesan (finely grated)
- 1 cup water

Ingredients (to Finish)

- ½ tbsp. everything bagel seasoning (or poppy seed/sesame seed mix)
- ½ tbsp. bacon (very finely chopped)
- ½ tbsp. pecans (very finely chopped)
- ½ tbsp. paprika (very finely chopped)

Instructions

1. Mix well egg whites and parmesan in a medium bowl until well blended like loose mashed potatoes.
2. Form into 4 balls and store in the refrigerator about 30 minutes to firm.
3. Roll 2 balls in each of the 4 ingredients to finish.
4. Set the balls in a steamer basket lined with parchment.
5. Add 1 cup of water into the Instant Pot with the steam rack inside. Then, carefully set the steamer basket on to the rack.
6. Tightly secure the lid in place with the vent release knob in the "Sealed" position. Select "Pressure Cook" / "Manual" and cook with the time set to 5 minutes using the "+/-" keys.
7. When the timer beeps, turn the knob to the "Venting" / "Vent" position for a quick-release of the pressure.
8. Then, serve warm.

Grandma's Pasta Salad

- **Prep Time:**   5 minutes
- **Cook Time:**   6 minutes
- **Yields:**   2 servings

Ingredients

- ¼ cup diced onion
- 1 ½ tbsp. sugar
- 1½ tbsp. vinegar
- 1¼ cup water
- 1 cup small pasta
- ½ tsp. salt
- ¼ cup mayo (or Miracle Whip)
- ½ tbsp. mustard
- ¼ tsp. celery seed
- Pinch salt to taste
- Pepper to taste
- ¼ cup chopped celery
- 1 oz. cheddar (diced)

Instructions

1. Mix the onion, sugar, and vinegar and then set aside.
2. Pour the water in the Instant Pot and add salt and pasta, stir very well.
3. Tightly secure the lid in place with the vent release knob in the "Sealed" position. Select "Pressure Cook" / "Manual" and cook with the time set to 5 minutes using the "+/-" keys.
4. When the timer beeps, flip the vent valve to the "Venting" / "Vent" position for a quick release of the pressure. When the pin drops, unlatch and open the lid. Then drain the pasta.
5. Whisk together all of the mayo, mustard, celery seed, pepper, and salt. Add the vinegar/onion mixture and stir. Then pour everything over the pasta.
6. Add the celery and diced cheese and stir well.
7. Keep in the fridge for several hours to flavor.

Buffalo Cauliflower Bites

- **Prep Time:**   5 minutes
- **Cook Time:**   2 minutes
- **Yields:**   2 servings

Ingredients

- 1 head cauliflower (cut into large pieces)
- ¼ cup buffalo hot sauce
- ½ cup water

Instructions

1. Pour the water into the Instant Pot with the steam rack inside.
2. Pour the cauliflower pieces in a medium glass bowl and add the buffalo hot sauce. Toss well to evenly coat. Lower the bowl onto the Instant Pot on top of the steam rack.
3. Secure the lid in place with the vent release knob in the "Sealed" position. Select "Pressure Cook" / "Manual" and set to cook for 5 minutes using the "+/-" keys.
4. Once the timer beeps, flip the vent valve to the "Venting" / "Vent" position for a quick release of pressure. When the float valve drops, unlatch and open the lid.
5. Serve in a plate with toothpicks to pick the bites.

Pull-Apart Pizza Bread

- **Prep Time:**   15 minutes
- **Cook Time:**   22 minutes
- **Yields:**   2 servings

Ingredients

- Cooking spray
- 1¼ cups all-purpose flour
- 2 tsp. baking powder
- ¼ tsp. salt
- ½ cup butter (chilled and divided)
- ½ cup milk
- 1 tbsp. Italian seasoning
- ½ tsp. chili powder
- ¼ tsp. garlic powder
- ½ cup parmesan cheese (grated)
- ¾ cup water
- ¼ cup pizza sauce

Instructions

1. Spray a Bundt pan with cooking spray. Set aside. Whisk together the flour and baking powder with salt in a medium bowl. Cut ¼ cup of butter into small cubes. Place into dry ingredients. Mix in the butter, using a fork, until dry ingredients become crumbly, about the size of peas.
2. Gradually pour in ½ cup of milk and mix until it forms a dough. After thoroughly cleaning your hands, knead the dough for about 10 minutes, until smooth. Pour the dough onto a floured surface, pat into a 10-inch round. Cut it up into 1-inch pieces. Set aside.
3. Combine Italian seasoning, chili, garlic powder, and parmesan in a zip-top bag. Mix by closing the bag and shaking. Place the pieces of dough into the bag and gradually knead the bag until each dough piece is coated in the spice mixture.
4. Transfer the pieces of dough into the greased Bundt pan; arrange evenly.
5. Now start the Instant Pot on the "Sauté" mode and pour in the remaining ¼ cup butter. Whisk until butter is melted. Press "Cancel" to turn off the Instant Pot and pour the butter over the pizza dough pieces in Bundt pan as a topping. Remove and clean the cooking pot.
6. Return the inset and put it back in the Instant Pot. Lower the trivet into the pot and pour water.
7. Using a paper towel and foil, cover the Bundt pan. Crimp edges to block water from entering. Carefully lower the pan into the pot, using a foil sling.
8. Secure the lid in place with the vent release knob in the "Sealed" position. Select "Pressure Cook" / "Manual" and set to cook for 21 minutes using the "+/-" keys.
9. Once the timer beeps, wait for 5 minutes of natural pressure release and then flip the release valve to "Vent" for a quick-release of the remaining pressure. When the float valve drops, unlatch and open the lid. Use the sling to remove the Bundt pan and also remove the foil and paper towel.
10. Allow it to cool on the rack for 5 minutes and then serve with pizza sauce as dipping.

Guacamole

- **Prep Time:**   15 minutes
- **Cook Time:**   0 minutes
- **Yields:**   2 servings

Ingredients

- 3 ripe avocados (to be halved and pitted)
- 2 Roma tomatoes (to be seeded and finely chopped)
- ¼ medium red onion (to be finely chopped)
- 1 - 2 Serrano chilies (to be finely chopped)
- ¼ cup fresh cilantro (finely chopped)
- ¼ cup Mexican crema (or sour cream, optional)
- Coarse salt (to taste)

Instructions

1. Peel the avocado and scoop out the flesh into a medium bowl. Lightly mash with a fork or potato masher.
2. Stir in the remaining ingredients.
3. Cover the bowl with an airtight plastic wrap and refrigerate.
4. Serve when you are ready.

"Roasted" Garlic

- **Prep Time:**   5 minutes
- **Cook Time:**   7 minutes
- **Yields:**   2-3 servings

Ingredients

- 1 cup water
- 2-3 garlic heads
- 1 ½ tbsp. olive oil

Instructions

1. Pour the water into the Instant pot with the trivet inside.
2. Cut off the top quarter of each garlic head (the end toward the tip, not the wider flat root end). This exposes some of the garlic cloves below.
3. Rub ½ tablespoon of olive oil onto the cut area of the garlic head. This allows the olive oil to sink and permeate the cloves, into the papery skins. Arrange the garlic heads in the trivet with the cut side up.
4. Lock the lid. If you are using the Max Pressure Cooker, select "Pressure Cook" set to cook on Max pressure for 5 minutes, the "Keep Warm" setting should be off.
5. If you're using All Pressure Cookers, select, "Pressure Cook"/ "Manual" and cook on High Pressure for 7 minutes, the "Keep Warm" setting should be off.
6. Once the timer beeps, wait for 20 minutes for natural pressure release. When the float valve drops, unlatch and open the cooker. Gently pick up each garlic head, using tongs, and transfer each head to a large plate. Allow it to cool for 5 minutes.
7. Now, squeeze the warm garlic cloves out of paper hulls. You can also cool for 1 hour to reach room temperature. Then seal their heads individually in plastic wraps. Refrigerate for up to seven days.

Loaded Bundt Cornbread

- **Prep Time:**   15 minutes
- **Cook Time:**   20 minutes
- **Yields:**   2-3 servings

Ingredients

- ¼ cup yellow cornmeal
- ¼ cup all-purpose flour
- ½ tsp. baking powder
- ½ tsp. granulated white sugar
- ¼ tsp. table salt
- ½ cups water
- 1 small egg at room temperature
- ¼ cup regular buttermilk
- ¼ cup frozen corn kernels (thawed)
- ¼ oz. semi-firm mozzarella (shredded)
- 1 tbsp. butter (melted and cooled to room temperature, and more added for greasing the pan)
- ¼ cup green chilies (hot or mild, chopped)

Instructions

1. In a small bowl, whisk together the cornmeal, all-purpose flour, baking powder, white sugar, and salt until uniform. Set aside.
2. Pour the water into the Instant Pot and set a trivet inside. Butter the inside of a Bundt pan and use an aluminum foil sling to set the pan in the pot.
3. In a small bowl, whisk together the egg and buttermilk until smooth and creamy. Stir in the butter, corn, chilies, and mozzarella. Now pour in the cornmeal mixture into the pot and stir until the cornmeal and flour are moistened become uniform throughout the batter.
4. Lay a paper towel on the Bundt pan and fold down the sling ends to fit into the cooker without having any contact with the paper towel.
5. Lock the lid in place. If you are using the Max Pressure Cooker, select "Pressure Cook" set to cook on Max pressure for 20 minutes, the "Keep Warm" setting should be off.
6. If you are using All Pressure Cookers, select, "Pressure Cook"/ "Manual" and cook on High Pressure for 25 minutes, the "Keep Warm" setting should be off.
7. Once the timer beeps to show the end of cook time, wait for 20 minutes for natural pressure release. When the float valve drops, unlatch and open the cooker. Gently transfer the Bundt to a wire rack to cool, using the aluminum sling you made. Remove the paper towel and let cool for about 5 to 10 minutes.
8. Unmold by setting a cutting board over the pan. Turn both the pan and cutting board upside-down and jiggle the pan for the cake to loosen. Then remove the pan and allow to continue cooling for about 10 minutes.
9. Slice into wedges and serve.

One-Pot Swedish Meatballs

- **Prep Time:** 20 minutes
- **Cook Time:** 20 minutes
- **Yields:** 2-3 servings

Ingredients (for Meatball Mixture)

- ¾ lb. ground beef (preferably 93% lean)
- ¼ cup panko bread crumbs
- ½ small onion (grated, with any juices)
- 1 small egg (to be beaten)
- 1 tbsp. finely chopped parsley
- ½ tsp. salt (or to taste)
- ½ tsp. garlic powder
- ¼ tsp. pepper
- ¼ tsp. allspice
- ¼ tsp. nutmeg

Ingredients (To Sauté)

- 1 tbsp. olive oil
- 1 tbsp. butter

Ingredients (for Sauce Mixture)

- 1 ¼ cups beef broth
- 2 tbsp. butter
- ½ cup cream
- ½ tsp. Dijon mustard
- ½ tbsp. Worcestershire

Ingredients (To Finish)

- ¼ cup cream
- ¼ cup flour
- Additional chopped parsley (for garnish)

Instructions

1. Combine all meatball mixture ingredients in a bowl and form into 15 meatballs. Set aside.
2. Start the Instant Pot on the "Sauté" function and add ingredients for sautéing when hot. Brown the meatballs in the melted butter and olive oil. Don't worry if the meats don't cook through this time. Transfer browned meat to a dish, cover loosely with foil. Add broth to the pot to deglaze using a wooden spoon to scrape the brown bits off the bottom of the pot.
3. Pour in the other sauce mixture ingredients and stir well to combine. Return the meatballs to the pot and ensure that all are coated in the sauce.
4. Select "Cancel" to turn off the pot with the vent release knob in the "Sealed" position. Select "Pressure Cook" / "Manual" and set to cook for 3 minutes using the "+/-" keys.

5. Once the timer beeps, wait for 7 minutes of natural pressure release and then flip the vent valve to "Vent" for a quick-release of the remaining pressure.
6. Carefully transfer the meatballs to a dish, cover loosely with foil.
7. In a small bowl, whisk together the remaining cream and flour. Add to the pot and stir. Let it simmer for about 3 to 5 minutes until thickened. Return to "Sauté" and adjust seasonings.
8. Serve as a side over egg noodles, mashed potatoes, or rice and garnish with chopped parsley.

Candied Cajun Trail Mix

- **Prep Time:**   5 minutes
- **Cook Time:**   17 minutes
- **Yields:**   2 servings

Ingredients

- 1 cup raw pecan halves
- 1 cup raw almonds
- 1 cup chickpeas (drained, or more if preferred)
- ¼ - ½ cup cashews
- ¼ cup raw sunflower seeds
- 2 - 3 tbsps. vegan butter (or regular butter)
- 1 tbsp. water (optional)
- ½ cup pure maple syrup
- ½ - 1 tbsp. spicy Cajun seasoning (or mix, you can also use ¼ to ½ tsp. each of cayenne pepper, garlic powder, onion powder, paprika, and red pepper powder)
- 1 pinch ground ginger
- 1 pinch sea salt (or to taste)
- 6 oz. dried mango (or spicy chili dried mango)

Instructions

1. Mix all ingredients thoroughly in the Instant Pot.
2. Start the Instant Pot on the "Sauté" function and keep stirring the ingredients with a plastic spatula for the butter to melt and nut/chickpeas to be coated with seasonings and maple syrup. Add 1 tablespoon of water if the batter is too sticky once sautéing.
3. Select "Pressure Cook" / "Manual" and set to cook for 10 minutes using the "+/-" keys.
4. Once the timer beeps, flip the valve to "Vent" for a quick-release of the pressure.
5. Transfer the nut mix onto a lined cooking sheet and spread. Preheat the oven to 375°F for 7-10 minutes and bake the nut, turning them halfway. Avoid burning the nuts.
6. Take it out of the oven and allow the Cajun trail mix to completely cool.

7. Then dice the mango into small pieces and add to the candied Cajun trail mix. Stir all well. (This can be done in ziplock or airtight container.)
8. You can add as more spices as you desire if you are using plain dried mango.
9. Store in an airtight container.

White Queso Party Dip

- **Prep Time:**   0 minutes
- **Cook Time:**   25 minutes
- **Yields:**   2-3 servings

Ingredients

- ¼ tsp. oil
- ¼ lb. ground turkey
- salt (or to taste)
- pepper (or to taste)
- ¼ cup water
- ¼ lb. white American cheese (sliced, from the deli)
- ¼ cup shredded Queso (Asadero or Queso quesadilla, or Monterey Jack)
- 1 ½ oz. canned tomato and chili mix (Ro-Tel, or more to taste, undrained)
- 1 oz. cream cheese
- 1 tsp. butter
- 1 tsp. milk
- ½ tsp. garlic powder
- ½ tsp. dried oregano
- Salsa and tortilla chips (or veggies, for serving)

Instructions

1. Start the Instant Pot with the "Sauté" function and add oil when the message "Hot" is displayed.
2. Brown the turkey in the heated oil, adding pepper and salt, until all pink disappears. Keep breaking as you continue sautéing.
3. Transfer the browned meat to a dish, drain and discard the liquids. Cover the dish loosely with foil.
4. Clean the Instant Pot by rinsing, then pour ¼ cup of water in the pot, insert the steam rack.
5. In a heat-proof casserole, mix the remaining ingredients. Carefully lower casserole.
6. Press "Cancel" to turn off the pot with the vent release knob in the "Sealed" position. Select "Pressure Cook" / "Manual" and set to cook for 15 minutes using the "+/-" keys.
7. Once the timer beeps, flip the vent valve to "Vent" for a quick-release of the pressure.

8. Add the cheese mixture and whisk until smooth. Stir in the turkey crumbles and adjust seasonings as needed.
9. Serve warm as a side to chips topped with a dollop of salsa or veggies.

Cilantro Lime Wings

- **Prep Time:**   0 minutes
- **Cook Time:**   30 minutes
- **Yields:**   2-3 servings

Ingredients

- 1 tbsp. olive oil
- ¾ - 1 lb. chicken wingettes
- 2 cloves garlic (minced)
- ¼ cup chicken broth
- 1½ tbsps. lime juice
- ¼ tsp. cayenne pepper
- ½ tsp. salt
- 1 tbsp. cilantro (chopped)
- Additional chopped cilantro (for garnish)

Instructions

1. Start the Instant Pot with the "Sauté" function and add olive oil when the message "Hot" is displayed.
2. Brown both sides of the chicken for 2-3 minutes per side. If the meat is not cooked through this time, never mind.
3. Add garlic and continue sautéing for about 2 minutes more. Return the chicken to the IP.
4. Add broth and lime juice to the pot to deglaze. Scrape all brown bits off from the bottom of the pot, using a wooden spoon.
5. Sprinkle with cayenne, salt, and cilantro without stirring.
6. Press "Cancel" to turn off the pot and turn the steam release knob to the "Sealed" position. Select "Pressure Cook" / "Manual" on the display panel and set to cook for 5 minutes using the "+/-" keys.
7. When the time is up and the timer beeps, allow 15 minutes for the natural pressure release, thereafter flip the steam release valve to "Vent" for a quick release of the pressure.
8. Carefully transfer the meat baking sheet lined with foil and broil for 5 minutes or until it turns golden brown.
9. Serve warm as a side to any grain, sprinkled with additional cilantro.

CHAPTER 9: THE INSTANT POT DESSERTS RECIPES FOR BEGINNERS

Desserts are as important as the main course when rating how enjoyable a meal has been. Many of the side dishes are partly serving as desserts in certain situations. That's why snacks, cakes, puddings, mousses, cookies, pecans, and creams, among others can be and should be prepared according to what they really are—desserts. All these and many more have been given as examples in this chapter so that you can have an idea of how to go about preparing your desserts. The recipes here, like those in the chapters before, are for just two.

Fudgy Chocolate Cake

- **Prep Time:**   15 minutes
- **Cook Time:**   30 minutes
- **Yields:**   2-3 servings

Ingredients (Dry)

- ½ cup sugar
- ½ tsp. vanilla
- ¼ cup butter
- 1 large egg
- ¼ cup flour
- ¼ cup cocoa powder
- ½ tsp. baking powder
- ¼ tsp. salt
- ½ cup chocolate chips
- ½ cup water
- Cooking spray

Instructions

1. Mix the sugar, vanilla, and butter well with an electric mixer in a large bowl until light and fluffy. Beat in the egg until well combined.
2. Whisk together the flour, baking powder, cocoa powder, baking powder, with salt. Then slowly combine the flour mixture and egg mixture until well blended. Add the chocolate chips and stir.
3. Spray a spring-form pan (preferably 8 inches) with a nonstick cooking spray. Add batter into the pan and smooth the top. Cover loosely with aluminum foil and set aside. Pour water into the Instant Pot with a wire trivet at the bottom. Then set the pan on top of the trivet. Cover with the lid and latch to lock with the vent sealed. Select "Pressure Cook"/ "Manual" and cook on High Pressure for 30 minutes.
4. After the cook time, allow 10 minutes for natural pressure release and then do a quick pressure release. Cut into wedges while still warm and serve when cool.

Homemade Crunchy Peach Crisp

- **Prep Time:**   5 minutes
- **Cook Time:**   30 minutes
- **Yields:**   2 servings

Ingredients (for Homemade Crunchy Peach Crisp)
- 2 cups frozen peach slices
- 1 tbsp. flour
- 1 tbsp. sugar
- ½ cup Water

Ingredients (for Topping Mixture)
- ¼ cup quick-cooking rolled oats
- ¼ cup brown sugar
- ¼ cup flour
- ¼ tsp. nutmeg
- ¼ cup pecans (chopped)
- ¼ cup butter (cut into 8 pieces)
- Ground cinnamon (for garnish, optional)

Instructions

1. Combine all ingredients for homemade crunchy peach crisp in a 6-cup Instant Pot-friendly casserole.
2. Pour water into the pot with steam rack inserted. Get a foil sling and use it to carefully position the casserole on the steam rack.
3. Put on the lid and tightly secure it in the place on the pot ensuring that the release knob is turned to the "Sealed" position.
4. On the display panel, select the "Pressure Cook" / "Manual" function and press the "+/-" keys to set the cook time to 20 minutes.
5. In the meantime, combine all of the ingredients for topping in a large nonstick skillet. Cook for 2-3 minutes over medium-high heat while you keep stirring.
6. Arrange 8 butter pieces to evenly dot the oat mixture and cook. Keep stirring until butter is melted and just fully incorporated.
7. Turn the oat mixture onto parchment paper immediately when it is still in a thin, even layer and allow to cool.
8. Once the Instant Pot beeps to indicate that the cooking time is up, wait for 5 minutes to let the pressure naturally release, then do a quick release of the remaining pressure.
9. Unlatch the pot to open the lid. Pour the oat as a topping on the peaches and arrange all an even layer. Press down a bit to give a good contact to the peaches. Wait for 5-10 more minutes for the mixture to set.
10. Take the casserole out of the Instant Pot and serve the peach crisp warm with cinnamon as a sprinkle.

Coconut-Blueberry Chia Pudding

- **Prep Time:**   10 minutes
- **Cook Time:**   3 minutes
- **Yields:**   2 servings

Ingredients

- 4 oz. full fat coconut milk
- ¼ cup water
- 3 oz. frozen blueberries
- ¼ cup chia seeds
- ¼ cup rolled oats
- ¼ cup pure maple syrup
- ¼ tsp. pure vanilla extract
- fresh berries (for garnish, optional)

Instructions

1. Combine the first seven ingredients on the recipe listing in the inner pot of the IP.
2. Put on the lid and tightly secure it in the place on the pot, ensuring that the release knob is turned to the "Sealed" position.
3. On the display panel, select the "Pressure Cook" / "Manual" function and use the "+/- " keys to set the cook time to 3 minutes on High Pressure.
4. After cooking, naturally release the pressure for 3 minutes, and then do a quick release of any remaining pressure.
5. Unlatch and remove the lid and pour the pudding into 2 serving cups. Keep in the fridge for about 1 hour or until it sets.
6. Then, serve cold with berries as the garnish. You may store in the refrigerator for up to 4 days if covered tightly.

Mixed Berry Mousse

- **Prep Time:**   5 minutes
- **Cook Time:**   40 minutes
- **Yields:**   2 servings

Ingredients

- 10 oz. frozen berries (2 cups, thawed, chosen from a combination of any of blackberries, blueberries, raspberries, or strawberries)

- 3 tbsps. sugar (divided)
- ½ tsp. finely grated lemon zest
- Pinch table salt (to taste)
- ¾ tsp. unflavored gelatin
- ¼ cup heavy cream
- 1 ½ oz. cream cheese (softened)

Instructions

1. Combine all berries, 1 ½ tablespoons of sugar, lemon zest, and table salt in a medium bowl. Leave for 30 minutes but keep stirring occasionally.
2. Place a fine-mesh strainer over another bowl and strain the berries. Pour the berries into the Ace Blender and set aside. Add 3 tablespoons of drained juice into a small bowl, sprinkle the gelatin on it, and allow it to sit for about 5 minutes until the gelatin softens.
3. In the meantime, microwave the remaining juice for 4-5 minutes or until reduced to about 3 tablespoons. Whisk gelatin mixture and the remaining 1 ½ tablespoon of sugar into reduced juice, mix until dissolved.
4. Cover the blender with the lid and lock. On medium speed, process the berries for about 30 seconds to smooth. Add the gelatin mixture, heavy cream, and softened cream cheese and return the lid. Then process again on medium speed for about 10 seconds. When it's well combined, increase the speed to High, then continue to process for about 30 seconds more or until smooth. Pause intermittently to scrape down all sides of the jar as often as needed.
5. Share the mousse into 2 serving dishes and cover each with a plastic wrap. Refrigerate for, at least, 4 hours to set or up to 2 days.
6. Then serve as a dessert.

Dulce De Leche

- **Prep Time:**   5 minutes
- **Cook Time:**   45 minutes
- **Passive Time:**   30 minutes
- **Yields:**   2 servings

Ingredients

- ½ can sweetened condensed milk (7 oz.)
- 1 cup water
- ½ tsp. sea salt (or to taste)
- Chopped almonds (for topping, optional)
- Chopped chocolate (for topping, optional)

Instructions

1. Prepare your ramekins (baking dish) by dividing the condensed milk evenly among the 2 ramekins, three inches in diameter. Tightly cover each ramekin with aluminum foil.
2. To pressure cook the Dulce de Leche, place the trivet or steam rack inside Instant Pot and pour water into the inner pot. Place the 2 ramekins on the trivet.
3. Put on the lid and tightly secure in place on the pot ensuring that the release knob is turned to the "Sealed" position.
4. On the display panel, select the "Pressure Cook" / "Manual" function and use the "+/-" keys to set the cook time to 45 minutes and adjust to cook on High Pressure.
5. When the cook time elapses, naturally release the pressure for 15 minutes, and then do a quick release of any remaining pressure.
6. Remove the ramekins carefully and then the foil. Sprinkle with the salt and leave to cool for 30 minutes.
7. Then top with optional chopped almonds and chopped chocolate and serve.

Slow Cooker - Giant Chocolate Chip Cookie

- **Prep Time:**   8 minutes
- **Cook Time:**   4 hours
- **Yields:**   2 servings

Ingredients

- Coconut oil spray
- ¼ cup erythritol and oligosaccharide blend (granular sweetener)
- 1 ½ tbsps. butter
- 1 small egg
- ¼ tsp. blackstrap molasses
- 1/8 tsp. vanilla extract
- 2/3 cup almond flour
- ¼ tbsp. coconut flour
- 2/3 tsp. baking powder
- 1/8 tsp. fine grind sea salt
- 1/8 tsp. xanthan gum
- 1/8 cup sugar-free stevia-sweetened (chocolate chips)
- 1/8 cup chopped walnuts

Instructions

1. Line the inner pot of the Instant Pot with parchment paper. Then spray with coconut oil spray (nonstick) and set aside.

2. Add the erythritol and oligosaccharide blend with butter to a large bowl. Cream the mixture thoroughly using a hand mixer or stand mixer, until well combined.
3. Combine the egg, blackstrap molasses, and vanilla extract and add. Continue to mix with the sweetener and butter mixture until thoroughly combined. Also set aside.
4. Add the almond flour and coconut flour with baking powder plus sea salt and xanthan gum in another bowl. Stir until blended.
5. Now combine both the dry ingredients and the wet ingredients. Mix thoroughly until a dough is formed. Fold in the sweetened chocolate chips and chopped walnuts.
6. Add the dough to the inner pot lined with the parchment paper. Use a rubber spatula to spread and press the dough to reach the bottom of the pot. Make sure that the entire bottom of the pot is completely covered, and fill in any gaps.
7. Cover the pot and lock the lid with the steam release handle in the "Venting" position. On the display panel, select the "Slow Cook" function on High and using the "+/-" button, program the pot to cook for 4 hours. You can go anywhere you like.
8. Simply press "Cancel" to turn off the pot when the cook time up.
9. Carefully open the lid and transfer the inner pot to a cooling rack with the cookie inside. Wait for a minimum of 30 minutes to allow the cookie cool in the pot to the room temperature. The cookie will continue to firm up as it cools.
10. Transfer the cookie to a serving plate, slice into equal-sized wedges, and serve warm. You may store in a resealable container and keep in the fridge for up to 6 days.

Apple Crisp

- **Prep Time:**   15 minutes
- **Cook Time:**   15 minutes
- **Yields:**   2 servings

Ingredients

- 2 cups apples (to be peeled, cored, and cut up)
- ¼ tsp. cinnamon
- ½ cup water
- ½ cup flour (any type, or more or less to taste)
- ½ cup oats
- ¼ cup brown sugar (or more or less to taste)
- 1/8 cup flax meal (ground flax seeds)
- ¼ cup butter (or more or less to taste)
- Dash of quality salt (to taste)

Instructions

1. Position the wire rack in the Instant Pot and set an oven-safe dish (like a 4 cup Pyrex dish) inside. Then add the water in the bottom.
2. Place the apple cuts into the dish. Sprinkle with the cinnamon.
3. Cover with the lid in the place and latch. On the display panel, select the "Pressure Cook"/ "Manual" function and have the pressure release valve turned to the "Sealing" position. Use the "+/-" button to set to cook for 6 minutes.
4. Meanwhile, preheat the oven to 370°F.
5. Combine the flour, oats sugar, and flax. Using a fork or pastry cutter, mix to have a crumble that can hold together when squeezed.
6. Set in the heated oven and bake to a golden brown, about 15 minutes. The granola-like crumble topping should stay together in clumps now.
7. When the Instant Pot beeps for time up, turn the release valve to the "Venting" position to do a quick release of the pressure.
8. The apples should be supper soft now on top and be somewhat crisp toward the bottom. Mix the apple to have the blend of the two texture, and then top with the finished crumb.
9. Serve and enjoy!

Warm Cinnamon Apples

- **Prep Time:**   10 minutes
- **Cook Time:**   10 minutes
- **Yields:**   2-3 servings

Ingredients

- 2 large honey crisp apples (to be peeled, cored and cut into about 6 slices)
- ½ tbsp. lemon juice
- ¼ cup water
- 1/3 cup brown sugar
- 1 tbsp. maple syrup
- ½ tbsp. cinnamon

Instructions

1. Toss the slices of apple with lemon juice in a large bowl.
2. Pour water into the Instant Pot and add in the apples.
3. Sprinkle the sugar, cinnamon, and maple syrup over the apples. Stir once to combine.
4. Cover with the lid in the place and latch. On the display panel, select the "Pressure Cook"/ "Manual" function and have the pressure release valve turned to the "Sealing" position. Use the "+/-" button to set to cook for 5 minutes.

5. When the Instant Pot beeps for time up, turn the release valve to the "Venting" position to do a quick release of the pressure.
6. Stir gently to mix. Serve alone as dessert, or over pound cake or ice cream.

Maple Candied Pecans

- **Prep Time:**   0 minutes
- **Cook Time:**   35 minutes
- **Yields:**   2 cups

Ingredients (for Syrup Mixture)
- ¼ cup pure maple syrup
- 1 tsp. cinnamon
- ½ tsp. vanilla
- ¼ tsp. ground ginger
- ¼ tsp. coarse salt (or to taste)
- 1/8 tsp. nutmeg
- 1/8 tsp. cayenne pepper (or to taste)
- 1/8 tsp. maple extract (optional)
- 2 cups pecan halves (about 10 oz.)
- 1/3 cup water

Ingredients (Sugar Finish Mixture)
- ¼ cup white sugar
- ¼ cup brown sugar
- ½ tsp. cinnamon

Instructions
1. Combine all of the 7 ingredients of syrup mixture on the listing, up to and including cayenne pepper, in the Instant Pot. Start the Instant Pot by putting it on the "Sauté" mode. Adjust to "More" or "High" on the panel and stir as the syrup cooks.
2. Stir in the pecans and cook and continue stirring for 5 minutes for pecans to be tender.
3. Pour in the water and stir to combine.
4. Select "Cancel" to turn off the pot off.
5. Cover with the lid in the place and latch. On the display panel, select the "Pressure Cook"/ "Manual" function and have the pressure release valve turned to the "Sealing" position. Use the "+/-" button to set to cook for 8 minutes.
6. Meanwhile, preheat the oven to 300°F.
7. Once the Instant Pot beeps for time up, turn the release valve to the "Venting" position to do a quick release of the pressure. Then stir to combine.

8. Use a slotted spoon to gently transfer pecans to the baking sheet lined with parchment in a single layer.
9. Now bake the pecan for 10 minutes. Stir to change sides and bake for another 5 minutes. Keep a watchful eye on it to avoid burning it.
10. To add the sugar mixture ingredients, take it out of the oven and allow to cool for 5 minutes. Add both the pecans and the mixture in a zip lock bag and shake well to coat.
11. Allow the pecan to cool, spread evenly on the parchment, before packaging and serving.

Cherry Clafoutis

- **Prep Time:** 10 minutes
- **Cook Time:** 20 minutes
- **Yields:** 2 servings

Ingredients

- Vegetable oil (as desired)
- 4 oz. pitted sweet cherries (frozen, ½ bag thawed and drained)
- 1 large egg
- ¼ cup sugar
- ¼ cup all-purpose flour
- ¼ cup whole milk
- 1/3 lemon zest
- Lemon juice (as much as can be extracted)
- 1/3 tsp. vanilla extract
- 1/3 cups water

Instructions

1. Rub a 6 × 4-inch baking pan with vegetable oil to moisture and pour the sweet cherries in the pan.
2. Combine the next 7 ingredients listed on the recipe listing, from the egg to vanilla extract, in a food processor. Process on low speed for about a minute, or on high speed for about 20 seconds, to be well combined and form a batter. Pour the mixture over the cherries and cover the pan tightly with aluminum foil, sealing it well on all sides.
3. Pour the water into the Instant Pot with a steamer rack or trivet inside. Lower the pan into the pot to be positioned on the rack.
4. Cover with the lid in the place and latch. On the display panel, select the "Pressure Cook"/ "Manual" function and have the pressure release valve turned to the "Sealing" position. Use the "+/-" button to set to cook for 20 minutes.
5. When the Instant Pot beeps for time up, leave it for 10 minutes to do the natural release of pressure and then quick-release the remaining pressure.

6. You may thereafter sprinkle with the additional sugar (if it remains) and bring to broil to lightly caramelize the clafoutis top (optional).
7. Then serve and enjoy.

Creme Brulee

- **Prep Time:**   5 minutes
- **Cook Time:**   6 minutes
- **Yields:**   2-3 servings

Ingredients

- 1 egg yolk
- ½ cup heavy whipping cream
- ½ tsp. vanilla extract
- ¼ cup Swerve confectioners (or more or less to taste)
- 1/8 tsp. salt (or more or less to taste)
- ½ cup filtered water

Instructions

1. Insert the trivet or a steam rack into the Instant Pot and pour the water.
2. Combine the egg yolks, heavy whipping cream, vanilla extract, confectioners, and salt in a bowl. Mix thoroughly and evenly pour into 2 or 3 well-greased, IP–friendly ramekins.
3. Carefully position the ramekins on the trivet. Cover each ramekin loosely with aluminum foil.
4. Cover with the lid in the place and latch. On the display panel, select the "Pressure Cook"/ "Manual" function and have the pressure release valve turned to the "Sealing" position. Use the "+/-" button to set to cook 6 minutes.
5. When the Instant Pot beeps for time up, leave it for about 10 minutes to do the natural release of pressure and then do a quick release of the remaining pressure.
6. Unlatch the lid and open. Then remove the ramekins, wait to let cool a bit.
7. Serve and enjoy!

Bourbon Sticky Toffee Pudding

- **Prep Time:**   10 minutes
- **Cook Time:**   35 minutes
- **Yields:**   2 servings

Ingredients

- ¼ cup Medjool dates (about 4 dates, chopped)

- 3 tbsps. hot water
- 1 tbsp. bourbon (or other types of whiskey)
- ¼ tsp. baking soda
- 1 ½ tbsp. butter
- 1 tbsp. milk
- ¼ cup flour
- ½ tsp. baking powder
- ¼ tsp. cinnamon
- 1/8 tsp. salt (or more or less to taste)
- Pinch nutmeg
- 1 small egg (beaten)
- Cooking spray
- ¾ cup water
- 1/8 cup caramel sauce (warmed)

Instructions

1. Combine chopped dates, hot water, whiskey (bourbon) and baking soda in a small bowl and set aside.
2. Combine butter and milk in another microwave-safe bowl. Microwave until butter is melted.
3. Add flour and baking powder with cinnamon, salt, and nutmeg to the milk and butter mixture and stir well until uniform.
4. Stir in the egg, bourbon and date mixture.
5. Coat the inside of 2 ramekins with nonstick cooking spray and pour the batter equally in the ramekins.
6. Cover the ramekins with foil coated in nonstick cooking spray (sprayed-side down).
7. Lower the steam rack or trivet into the Instant Pot and add water. Place the ramekins and their content on the steam rack.
8. Cover with the lid in the place and latch. On the display panel, select the "Steam" function and have the pressure release valve turned to the "Sealing" position. Use the "+/-" button to set to cook 20 minutes.
9. When the Instant Pot beeps for time up, leave it for about 10 minutes to do the natural release of pressure and then do a quick release of the remaining pressure.
10. Carefully take the ramekins out of the pot and run a knife around their edges to loosen the pudding and invert onto a serving dish.
11. Drizzle the caramel sauce on each pudding and serve warm.

Delightfully Baked Apples

- **Prep Time:**   10 minutes
- **Cook Time:**   15 minutes
- **Yields:**   2 servings

Ingredients (for Filling Mixture)

- 1/8 cup raisins
- 1/8 cup dates (chopped, alternatives are golden raisins, apricots, or prunes)
- 1/8 cup hazelnuts chopped
- 1 tsp. cinnamon
- 1 tbsp. brown sugar

Ingredients (for Delightfully Baked Apples)

- 2 small apples (any of empire, Honeycrisp, or Jonathan is preferable)
- 2 tbsp. butter
- 1/3 cup water

Instructions

1. Combine the 5 filling mixture ingredients in a small bowl and mix.
2. Using a paring knife or melon baller, remove the core of the apples, but leave their bottom ½-inch intact.
3. Fill apple cavities with the filling mixture and top each apple with a thin slice of butter.
4. Pour the water in the Instant Pot and set the 2 apples in the bottom. If any butter remains, add it to the cooking water.
5. Cover with the lid in the place and latch. On the display panel, select the "Pressure Cook" / "Manual" function and have the pressure release valve turned to the "Sealing" position. Use the "+/-" button to set to cook 3 minutes.
6. When the Instant Pot beeps for time up, leave it for about 5 minutes to do the natural release of pressure (if you desire extra-tender apples, leave for 10 minutes) and then do a quick release of the remaining pressure.
7. Serve warm.

S'Mores Brownies

- **Prep Time:**   5 minutes
- **Cook Time:**   55 minutes
- **Yields:**   2 servings

Ingredients

- 1 graham cracker
- 1/3 cup brownie batter (prepared)
- 1/8 oz. Hershey chocolate bar (roughly chopped, 2 rectangles)

- 1/3 cup water
- 2 marshmallows (not miniature)

Instructions

1. Lay a parchment paper in the rectangular shape on the bottom of a loaf pan.
2. Add the graham cracker into the pan, right on the parchment paper.
3. Divide the prepared brownie batter into two and spread ½ of it over the graham cracker. Then sprinkle the chopped chocolate over the batter.
4. Top with remaining ½ of the prepared brownie batter and cover loosely with foil (don't seal).
5. Pour 1/3 cup of water into the pot and insert the steam rack. Then carefully lower the loaf pan onto the pot to be positioned on the steam rack.
6. Cover with the lid in the place and latch. On the display panel, select the "Pressure Cook" / "Manual" function and have the pressure release valve turned to the "Sealing" position. Use the "+/-" button to set to cook 35 minutes
7. When the time Instant Pot beeps for time up, leave it for about 10 minutes to do the natural release of pressure and do a quick release of the remaining pressure.
8. Take the loaf pan our and top with 2 marshmallows. Place under the broiler for about 3 minutes or until golden brown. (Keep checking to avoid burning)
9. Use a fork to lightly flatten the marshmallows so that they can spread.
10. Wait for at least 10 minutes to allow it cool.
11. Run a knife through the edge of the pan, loosen and remove from pan.
12. Cut into two and serve.

CONCLUSION

The Instant Pot has taken the cooking beyond speed and mere doneness. The focus and attention have graduated. They are all about tastes these days. All of us have come to the realization that our meals taste better when they're pressure cooked. This explains the growing interest in this pressure cooker. In reality, given the same ingredients and leveling all other factors except the pot, food pressure cooked in the Instant Pot will beat all other ones cooked elsewhere.

Nevertheless, it still boils down to culinary skills as said earlier. What on earth will make you realize the need for the Instant Pot in the first place? It's your exposure and experience in cooking that tells you what each cooking utensil can help you achieve. But what if you don't know how to use the Instant Pot and you've got to cook in it? You run a high risk of messing up your recipe.

Does it sound somehow pedestal that someone needs to understand the use of the Instant Pot? Users' experiences have demonstrated this. Oh wait! Even you! What have you read in this book? Has it not opened your eyes to a few more or many more things about your Instant Pot? That's why this cookbook refuses to limit itself to taking you through only lists of recipes and what to do with them.

Of course, you have read about over 100 recipes cutting across different categories of foods in this book. Many of these are unique while a good number of them are what you've known but would still want to have around your table any time. You have seen that in this cookbook, the recipes that you might have considered common have been given some unique twists and tweaks which translate them into meals with special tastes.

What you will do with what you learn here ultimately belongs to you.

Yummie!

APPENDIX: ABBREVIATIONS, MEASUREMENTS & CONVERSIONS

Abbreviations

This cookbook has been written with those new to the Instant Pot in mind. Thus, certain expressions were spelled out. Nevertheless, exigencies demand the use of abbreviations in certain contexts. Some other cookbooks are superfluous in the use of abbreviations. So that you don't get confused about abbreviations you come across here or in other books about the Instant Pot, the appendix has been prepared to show you the commonest of them.

1. **IP:** This refers to the Instant Pot itself. Some call it Magic Pot.
2. **Pothead:** Also known as potters. This refers to the Instant Pot users.
3. **PC:** Pressure Cookers. This is the general description of cooking pots that cook with high pressure.
4. **EPC:** Electric Pressure Cooker. The Instant Pot is one brand among many of this.
5. **HP:** High Pressure. This is the pressure in the pot when you cook at 10.2 – 11.6 psi.
6. **LP:** Low Pressure. This is the pressure in the pot when you cook at 5.8 – 7.2 psi.
7. **NR:** Natural Release. This is what you do when you don't touch the Instant Pot after a cooking cycle. The pressure will go down and the floating valve will naturally drop eventually.
8. **NPR:** Natural Pressure Release. It is the same thing as NR.
9. **QR:** Quick Release, also known as Manual Release. This is what you do when you turn the venting knob/ handle/ valve from the sealed/sealing position to the vent/venting position. This is usually done after a specified amount of time of the NPR or without first doing the NPR. QR allows all the pressure to be released manually and quickly while the pin drops.
10. **QPR:** Quick Pressure Release. This is the same as QR.
11. **HA:** High Altitude. Location of the cooking influences the time it takes for the Instant Pot to reach pressure and the optimal cook time. Those living in high altitudes (about 3000 ft. above sea level) need to adjust the cooking times for most recipes.
12. **PIP:** Pot in Pot / Pan in Pan. This is a benefit of the Instant Pot that enables you to cook more than one dish at the same time in the same pot if they have a similar cook time. It requires having different small oven-safe pots.

13. **5-5-5**: High Pressure: 5 minutes, Natural Pressure Release: 5 Minutes, Ice Bath: 5 Minutes. It is a way of recommending timing for the above when cooking eggs. It may also be given as 6-6-6.

14. **SS**: Stainless Steel. This is used when you are describing the material used in making an Instant Pot.

15. **SSB**: Stainless Steel Bowl. This refers to the pot that you can place directly inside the Instant Pot to cook. The size of the SSB depends on the size of the pot.

16. **SB**: Steamer Basket. If you need a basket to steam foods inside the Instant Pot SSB.

17. **PSI**: Pound Per Square Inch. This is the measurement of the atmospheric pressure. The measurement of the pressure inside the Instant Pot is given in PSI.

Measurements

This Instant Pot comes mainly in the sizes, namely 3 quarts, 6 quarts, and 8 quarts. Even though insignificant, the difference in sizes of Instant pots translates to different cooking times.

It takes longer for bigger-size Instant Pot to come to pressure. However, once the pot comes to the pressure, the cook time for each recipe is essentially the same.

Wattage

It's also good to note the wattage for each size. The understanding of this will let you know how quickly it will come to pressure and the heat it will produce.

- 3 quarts Instant Pot means 700 Watts
- 6 quarts Instant Pot means 1000 Watts
- 8 quarts Instant Pot means 1200 Watts

Inner Liner Diameter

Another measurement that gives you an insight into the functionality of your pot is the diameter of the inner liner of the IP.

- The diameter of the inner pot of 3 quarts Instant Pot is 7 inches
- The diameter of the inner pot of 6 quarts Instant Pot is 8.5 inches
- The diameter of the inner pot of 8 quarts Instant Pot is 9.25 inches

Liquid Content

As t has been observed, the Instant Pot generally requires just a small amount of water or any cooking liquid. Take the following as a rule of thumb.

- The 3 quarts Instant Pot requires ¾ of liquid
- The 6 quarts Instant Pot requires 1 cup of liquid
- The 8 quarts Instant Pot requires 1 ½ cups of liquid

Conversions

The following units of measurement are given in this book

- Lb symbolizes Pounds
- Oz symbolizes Ounces
- Tsp.(s) symbolizes teaspoon(s)
- Tbsp.(s) symbolizes tablespoon(s)
- 1 cup = 48 teaspoons, 16 tablespoons
- 1 quart = 32 ounces

However, it's more important to have an idea of the difference in cook time between the IP and a slow cooker or oven and stovetop. You can use this sample in understanding what to expect as the cook time for each recipe.

Converting From Slow Cooker to the Instant Pot

Cook Time on Slow Cooker	Cook Time on the IP
10 hours on low or 5 hours on high	30 minutes on high pressure
8 hours on low or 4 hours on high	24 minutes on high pressure
6 hours on low or 3 hours on high	18 minutes on high pressure
4 hours on low or 2 hours on high	12 minutes on high pressure

Converting From Oven or Stovetop to the Instant Pot

Cook Time on Oven or Stove	Cook Time on the IP
2 hours	40 minutes on high pressure
1 ½ hours	30 minutes on high pressure
1 hour	20 minutes on high pressure
½ hour	10 minutes on high pressure

Take the pasta to illustrate this.

General Pasta Cook Time	Pasta Cook Time on the IP
12 minutes	4 minutes on high pressure (5 minutes of NPR then QR)
9 minutes	3 minutes on high pressure (4 minutes of NPR then QR)

6 minutes	2 minutes on high pressure (3 minutes of NPR then QR)
3 minutes	1 minute on high pressure (2 minutes of NPR then QR)

Consider other common examples in the table below

Food	Slow Cooker Cook	Instant Pot Cook
Beef (roast)	8-10 hours on low	15 minutes
Beef (stew)	8-10 hours on low	15-20 minutes
Ground beef	4-6 hours on low	5 minutes
Meatballs	4-6 hours on low	10-15 minutes
Chicken breast	4-6 hours on low	6 minutes
Chicken thighs (bone-in)	6-8 hours on low	10 minutes
Chicken thighs	6-8 hours on low	8 minutes
Whole chicken	6-8 hours on low	6 minutes
Pork chops (bone-in)	8 hours on low	8 minutes
Pork chops (boneless)	8 hours on low	5 minutes
Pork shoulder (3	8 hours on low	55 minutes
Pork lion (2 - 3 pounds)	10 hours on low	20-25 minutes
Fish fillet	1-2 hours on low	5 minutes
Meatloaf	7-8 hours on low	20-25 minutes
White rice	1-2 hours on low	5 minutes
Whole potatoes	8 hours on low	14 minutes

Made in the USA
Coppell, TX
08 December 2019

12604432R00081